"Let's confront the unpleasant reality and say it out loud, AA doesn't work for many of the people struggling to overcome alcohol and other drug problems, and yet there continue to be precious few treatment alternatives. Don't despair if you've tried the traditional route and failed. Follow James DeSena's suggestions for *Overcoming Your Alcohol, Drug and Recovery Habits* and find your own path to sobriety."
—Scott D. Miller, Ph.D., author of *Working with the Problem Drinker* and *The Miracle Method: A Radically New Approach to Problem Drinking*

"If you have doubts about what happens in 12-step oriented treatment, and no place to turn for a fresh perspective, this book is for you!"
—A. Thomas Horvath, Ph.D., FAClinP, President of SMART Recovery, author of *Sex, Drugs, Gambling & Chocolate: A Workbook for Overcoming Addictions*

"This book is incredibly well written, thoughtful, truthful, and incisive. The method Jim outlines for discovery instead of recovery is inspired. I hope many who are not satisfied with AA and its program will read his book and find answers to some of their questions. This book is a wonderful addition to the literature on alternatives to AA as well as exposing some of the harder truths behind the AA message."
—Marianne Gilliam, author of *How Alcoholics Anonymous Failed Me*

"Jim DeSena's powerful 'quit for good' abstinence approach short-circuits distorted thinking and empowers addicted pesons to reclaim their lives. This book celebrates freedom-from-addiction alternatives and is a welcome addition to the alcoholism lierature."
—James Christopher, founder of Secular Organizations for Sobriety, author of *How to Stay Sober* and *SOS Sobriety*

"*Overcoming Your Alcohol, Drug and Recovery Habits* does a fine job of exposing the lies and harmful effects of AA and 12-step treatment. This book will provide a welcome ray of hope to the many, many individuals who have gone through AA and 12-step treatment, yet continue to relapse. It will help them get off the exceptionally destructive 'recovery' merry-go-round and retake control of their own lives."
—Charles Bufe, author of *Alcoholics Anonymous: Cult or Cure?*, co-author of *Resisting 12-Step Coercion: How to Fight Forced Participation in AA, NA, or 12-Step Treatment*

Overcoming Your Alcohol Drug and Recovery Habits

An Empowering Alternative to AA and 12-Step Treatment

James DeSena

See Sharp Press • Tucson, Arizona • 2003

For information contact See Sharp Press, P.O. Box 1731, Tucson, AZ 85702.
E-mail: info@seesharppress.com
Web site: http://www.seesharppress.com

DeSena, James, 1956.
Overcoming your alcohol, drug, and recovery habits : an empowering alternative to AA and 12-Step treatment / James DeSena ; with an introduction by Joseph Gerstein, MD. – Tucson, AZ : See Sharp Press, 2003.
    188 p. ; 23 cm.
    Includes bibliographical references and index.
    ISBN 1-884365-29-9

    1. Alcoholism — Treatment — Evaluation. 2. Drug abuse — Treatment — Evaluation. 3. Alcoholics Anonymous. 4. Twelve-step Programs. 5. Self-help techniques. I. Title.
                   616.8606

For Leanna and Anthony,
that they may always know freedom

Contents

Introduction

by Joseph Gerstein, M.D.

I am a physician. If a patient of mine turned out to have a cancerous breast lump of a certain common type, I would sit with her and discuss in detail her options for treatment. The options would, naturally, be based on an up-to-date assessment of the information available in the medical literature and would include modified radical mastectomy (surgical removal of the breast) and lumpectomy (removal of the lump with a modest amount of normal tissue around it) followed by radiation therapy. Medical research has demonstrated that either approach would have the same outcome in terms of survival. A middle-aged woman with severe emphysema or a frail elderly woman with multiple, severe medical problems might receive the added option of doing nothing, on the presumption that either treatment might be more likely to be detrimental than doing nothing.

Any deviation from this general scenario would likely result in a disciplinary action by the state Board of Medical Licensure. A physician who offered only one of the two options would probably even have his or her license summarily suspended pending a hearing on more severe sanctions, so heinous a deviation from ethical medical behavior would this be considered.

Yet, this very scenario will be enacted a thousand times daily, all over America, as people with severe alcohol problems seek or are coerced to seek advice about treatment in offices, clinics, emergency units and detoxification units.

We have a situation in which both licensed professionals and laypeople with only their personal experience in overcoming alcohol dependence and informal training, either through ignorance or fanatic zeal or stubbornness or monolithic training, offer only one treatment option to their clients despite prodigious amounts of scientific evidence that many other reasonable alternatives exist and make no attempt whatsoever to determine which of these might offer the greatest opportunity for success, which might coincide with the client's religious beliefs (or non-beliefs) and/or temperamental peculiarities or preferences.

I should know. For the first 20 years of my medical practice career, that is exactly what I did. That's how I was trained. That's what I was told. And that's what I did . . . out of ignorance, not out of malice.

Now I know better. Jim DeSena, in this volume, delineates clearly and in detail that this "one size fits all" approach to alcohol abuse and dependence is as archaic as leech application. It is time for the healing professionals to get over this "Berlin Wall" mentality and open themselves to the bright light of thousands of outcome studies (including the huge MATCH study) which amply demonstrate that there is more than one way to skin a cat.

Also, as Jim DeSena demonstrates, the fundamental Hippocratic precept "First, Do No Harm," is also abrogated on a daily basis. There are those who are harmed by the inappropriate referral because they lose precious time, during which their lives continue to unravel, perhaps never to be raveled again. There are those who decide to resist the prescribed treatment, which they perceive as alien and therefore get no appropriate treatment. And, there are those who come to be convinced to accept beliefs, which lead them to believe they are incorrigible, beliefs which are inapplicable to them and will permanently prevent them from recovering because of this factor alone.

This is a perverse train of events. Just because a treatment may be proper and effective for some people does not mean that it must be good for everyone. Medical studies usually require a "control" group because it is recognized that practically all treatments have a propensity for negative results as well as positive and that failure of the treatment is not automatically attributable to the bad intentions or incompetence of the patient. And what about all those, probably the majority, who will recover spontaneously. Must they, too, be condemned to a life of daily meetings and to carry the disparaging descriptor "alcoholic" for the rest of their natural lives even if they don't ever drink alcohol again?

Jim DeSena's excellent book is one more cogent and eloquent plaint for a rational, humane and scientifically validated approach to proper matching of clients with addiction problems to treatment appropriate for them.

—Joseph Gerstein, M.D., FACP
Harvard Medical School

Preface
An Old Story and New Beginning

Sitting in silence, Robert damned himself for relapsing again. This was his fifth rehab. He knew what lay ahead: Twenty-eight days of very expensive AA meetings. While the admissions counselor completed the paper work, Robert spied a wall plaque:

Insanity: Continuing to do the same thing over and over while expecting different results.

Robert slumped deeper in his chair. He knew this definition well. He first heard it in a TV commercial for a treatment center. The tough-talking pitch man used it to demonstrate the "insanity" of repeated alcohol/drug use despite the serious negative consequences. Robert agreed. If ever there was a word to describe his boozing, insanity was it. Drink after drink—the results were always the same—drunk after drunk.

Robert started thinking, but his thoughts were cut short. "Sign right here," the counselor droned, tapping a line with a pen. "We have your old room ready," he said. Was that a half grin?

Pen in hand, Robert looked hard at the counselor.

"Anything wrong," asked the counselor looking at his watch. "I have three more I need to process before lunch."

"Hell yes," Robert answered as he slammed down the pen. "Something's very wrong. Insanity!" The counselor's eyebrows rose.

Robert pointed to the plaque, "Doesn't that definition apply to going through treatment over and over, but expecting different results?" Robert was heading for rehab number five and he knew others who had hit double digits. Treatment after treatment—the results were always the same—relapse after relapse. "Maybe we're all crazy," the counselor countered, "but we can be restored to sanity when we get treatment and start recovering."

"Treatment! Recovery!" Robert cried out. "You're gonna keep me here for a month, tell me I'm diseased and powerless, and then tell me to stick with AA, get a new sponsor, work the program, and connect with some higher power."

"I have a better idea," said Robert, heading for the door. "I'm quitting booze for good."

"That's your disease talking," the counselor said mechanically. "You can't quit for good, none of us can. That's why we're always recovering—we need meetings."

"No! That's insane!" Robert shot back. "People quit cigarettes and knock off all kinds of addictions without meetings, don't they? You can live in recovery if you want to, but I'm through with boozing and recovery."

The counselor blinked, squirmed and then stared at the unsigned paper as Robert walked out the door.

In fact, the "insanity" label applied to your compulsive behaviors also fits the compulsive behaviors of people who recycle you through the same treatment, despite its consistent failure. Their "insanity" becomes glaringly apparent once you discover that you can quit for good, without their "help." It's clear that a new definition is called for:

> Insanity: 12-step addiction treatment and lifelong "recovery," that is, doing the same thing over and over while expecting different results, despite its lack of efficacy and obvious negative, and sometimes deadly, consequences.

Studies clearly show that nearly 80% of people who quit booze and other drugs do so without any treatment. But misguided addiction counselors and therapists ignore this fact to keep you on the treatment treadmill and forever "recovering." They profit by ineffectively treating a nonexistent "disease." Worse, even though they view alcoholism/addiction as a disease, their "treatment" consists of spiritual/religious indoctrination. Even they admit that this cures nothing. Instead, they claim that with divine help you're granted a one-day-at-a-time addiction reprieve.

It's important to note that AA and the 12-step approach of addiction treatment are not exactly the same. In theory, AA meetings are supposed to be independent, self-supporting, and not associated with any sect, denomination or institution. While a rehab/hospital may bring in AA speakers and provide meeting space, unless rehab/hospital staff step outside their professional roles as counselors and supervisors and participate as recovering alcoholics or drug addicts, they cannot run AA-sanctioned meetings in their facilities. If staff members run meetings in their professional capacity, and not as recovering alcoholics or addicts, they are technically running 12-step meetings, which are effectively the same as AA meetings except that donations are not requested.

Having made this distinction, be aware that I will use the terms AA meetings and 12-step meetings interchangeably.

Pop psychology and faith healing have been highly profitable for ages. One form they take is that of alcohol/drug treatment. As an alternative to this, *Overcoming Your Alcohol, Drug and Recovery Habits* presents the easily understood methods used by people who have successfully quit addictions/dependencies on their own. You can quit for good—without therapists, counselors, rehabs, sponsors and a lifetime of recovery meetings.

For Good?

If you're seeking a healthier, happier way of life, free from the bondage of booze, quitting for good makes sense. Yet, please note that many alcohol abusers, even alcoholics, beat their booze problem by learning to moderate. Some will do this on their own; others will seek support through moderation counselors/therapists or moderation programs.

Moderation programs, though, are anathema to disease theory advocates. "Alcoholics" aren't supposed to be able to control their drinking—ever. According to disease theory dogma, one drink sets the "craving" phenomenon into motion, leading to yet another drinking debacle. Yet the mere existence of organizations such as Moderation Management, Drink/Link and DrinkWise provides powerful evidence that their members have found a successful alternative to abstinence.

For some people however, the strict drinking guidelines of moderation programs are so demanding that it's simply easier for them to stay away from booze altogether. Many adjust to moderation with relative ease. Those who cannot, in the spirit of self-interest, often decide to quit for good. In fact, those who initially set a moderation goal and fail to achieve it often do succeed at abstaining once they decide to do so.

While I've written *Overcoming Your Alcohol, Drug and Recovery Habits* for those who want to quit drinking or abusing other drugs entirely, this is a book about choices. You are free to try moderation programs and decide if moderation is a viable option for you. Please see Appendix B for more information on moderation.

Key Words

Language used in the addictions field is laden with caveats and often leads to serious misunderstandings. Such polarizing labels as "alcoholic," "alcohol abuser," "alcohol dependent," "heavy drinker," "chemically dependent," "drug addict," "drug dependent," and "drug abuser" contribute to the myths surrounding substance addiction and how to overcome it. This book exposes these myths and provides insights into many recovery buzzwords.

You don't have to label yourself to quit for good—you are much more than an "alcoholic," or a "drug addict."

Please familiarize yourself with the following key words:

Addiction: Compulsive and overwhelming involvement with a specific activity. Continuing this behavior despite knowing the severe personal and social havoc it causes. The activity may be gambling, Internet surfing or may involve the use of almost any substance. Physically addictive substances such as tobacco and heroin can cause either psychological dependence or both psychological and physical dependence.

Addict: A person actively practicing addiction.

Alcoholic: A person actively addicted to alcohol.

Alcoholism: A behavior/lifestyle characterized by a tendency to drink more than was intended, unsuccessful attempts at stopping drinking, and continued drinking despite adverse social, personal, and occupational consequences.

Chemical Dependence: A state of psychological or physical dependence, or both, categorized by a withdrawal syndrome. The experience of physical or psychological reactions, or both, when use of the drug/alcohol is discontinued.

Traditional Recovery: Remission from the hypothetical disease alcoholism/addiction—a state of tentative sobriety. Maintaining this requires the guidance of sponsors and a Higher Power acquired through membership in 12-step groups. These groups, sponsors and Higher Powers provide a spiritual force, which keeps the allegedly incurable, progressive disease at bay.

Traditional Treatment: A procedure that uses the 12-step program of Alcoholics Anonymous to treat a hypothetical progressive disease (alcoholism/addiction) that cannot be cured. Treatment can be either inpatient or outpatient and is intended to lead the client to a tentative state of sobriety called "recovery." Such treatment teaches the patient to "work the program," aided by sponsors and the wisdom, courage and serenity flowing from supernatural forces, that is, a Higher Power. Follow-up treatment termed "aftercare" reinforces the clients' powerlessness and perceived need for divine help.

Now let's introduce two new important terms:

Discovery: Living life free from addiction, recovery and treatment. No steps, sponsors, counselors, rehabs, meetings or program to work. You decide for yourself how you will live your life. This means freedom to experience and live life on your own terms.

Self-Discovered: A term describing people who learn, or intuitively know, how to quit and stay away from alcohol, other drugs, and other addictions. Anyone can learn to do this, despite the damage caused by prior addiction treatment and recovery group (AA) involvement.

Know these abbreviations. They are detailed in Chapter 1:

ATI: Addiction Treatment Industry
RGM: Recovery Group Movement

Throw Away the Training Wheels

Alcohol is a socially accepted drug, so it is culturally set apart from other, illegal drugs. Wine-tastings and cocktail hours are common social events. But pharmacologically, alcohol is a drug, just as heroin, cocaine and methamphetamine are drugs. Unless I refer to the drug alcohol specifically, the words "alcohol" and "drug" are interchangeable. You'll also see "alcohol/drugs," which means "alcohol and other drugs."

Through research, personal experience and information gathered from others who have quit on their own, I have acquired the techniques you'll need to remain alcohol/drug/recovery-free for the rest of your life. Once you discover what you're actually up against, quitting alcohol and other drugs will become a learned skill well within your ability, like learning to ride a bicycle. Yes, you'll be a bit wobbly at first, but once you've learned—it's over! There's no need for daily practice—or one-day-at-a-time recovery. Best of all, this automatic skill will be there when you need it—which will be less and less often, because addiction and recovery-free living become self-perpetuating. And with addictions out of the way, "living life on life's terms," to quote AA, is not the meeting after meeting recovery process it's made out to be.

Discovering rather than recovering gives you two more gifts, freedom and time—no more "working the program" and bouncing from meeting to meeting, from sponsor to counselor. You can now live your own life. Spiritual and self-improvement projects are not required to quit any addiction. They will be your choice to pursue when you want, with whom you want, and if you want—not because you have to pursue them as the means to get and stay sober.

This Is Your Moment

People overcome addictions every day. They were doing it long before Alcoholics Anonymous and today's addiction experts began telling them they couldn't. America's multi-billion-dollar addiction treatment industry (ATI) stresses, "You can't do it alone" and "Treatment works." If treatment works so well, why do people check into rehab four, five, six times and more? Why are we constantly reading about sports stars and other celebrities heading toward the same dismal fate, over and over? How can you avoid a similar destiny? In truth, the ATI's catch phrase, "treatment works," means, "treatment rarely works."

Overcoming Your Alcohol Drug and Recovery Habits answers the preceding questions, taking a hard look at the addiction treatment industry and its problematic solution to what is touted as a disease: alcoholism/addiction. The goal of this book is twofold: to help you achieve freedom from lifelong addiction *and* from recovery.

Because of AA's overwhelming presence in the addiction/recovery field, revealing its ineffectiveness is necessary. This book makes clear the damage from the "It's our way, or the highway" crusade.

Undoubtedly, recovery traditionalists will cry, "AA bashing" while denying the truth. But perhaps, just perhaps, they will finally face reality:

> All truth passes through three stages: First, it is ridiculed. Second, it is violently opposed. Third, it is accepted as self-evident.
> —Arthur Schopenhauer

Until 12-step traditionalists break through their denial, they will question my character, not my message. They will brand me a charlatan, a book-selling profiteer, and they will ignore the fact that I'm offering people a solid way out of addiction.

In fairness though, for those it does help, AA is a beacon of hope, something they wouldn't trade for the world. These folks go on to lead sober, productive lives and are happy in the fellowship. People from all walks of life, all religions—even no religion—wouldn't trade their affiliation with AA for the world. They find it a satisfying way of life. But countless individuals are not as fortunate. For those in need of alternative recovery methods, this book may well be their beacon of hope. The point is that AA offers a recovery program, which for most people is the wrong program. It doesn't help them. For this reason, alternatives must be considered. It's time to recognize some of the harsher truths behind the AA message. To deny anyone an alternative is to deny him or her the chance for a sober, fulfilling life.

I've written *Overcoming Your Alcohol, Drug and Recovery Habits* for those suffering in ineffective addiction treatment programs and recovery groups. It's for those who want to end their addictive behaviors *now*, not attend meetings for the rest of their lives. The family and friends of substance abusers will also benefit as they learn what they can do to help themselves along with helping their addicted loved one. You are about to embark on an empowering journey of discovery that recovery cannot give you. Learn form the real treatment experts: people who have quit addictions on their own. Like them, you will learn to be free from addiction and recovery.

If you want to quit booze/drugs for good, this book is for you. If you're considering quitting, this book will help you decide.

There's no need to recover. It's time to discover.

—James DeSena, July, 2002

Acknowledgements

My thanks go to Dr. Jeffrey A. Schaler, a trailblazer in the alternative 12-step arena. Thank you for your encouragement. To Dr. Joseph Gerstein, whose observant eye and enthusiasm for this project have both aided and encouraged me. Thank you for writing the Introduction.

I am also very grateful to Dr. Stanton Peele, Dr. Thomas A. Horvath, Dr. Philip Tate, Dr. Scott D. Miller, James Christopher, CAS, Richard Dowling, MA, MAC, and Marianne Gilliam. Their thoughtful feedback on earlier versions of the manuscript have helped me make *Overcoming Your Alcohol, Drug and Recovery Habits* a much stronger book.

A special thank you to Sharon Naylor, a gifted writer whose passion for the written word inspired me to forge ahead with this venture. Laudations are in order for all the former substance abusers who have shared with me their "secrets" of addiction- and recovery-free living.

On a very personal note, I need to acknowledge my brother, Tony. His editorial suggestions, patience, insights and his selfless donation of his time and energy go beyond words. Thank you my brother.

Finally, to the rest of my beloved family; all of you mean the world to me.

Chapter 1

Trick or Treatment?

The early morning quiet was shattered when Brynn Hartman, wife of actor Phil Hartman, shot Phil and then turned the gun on herself. She was recovering after drug and alcohol treatment. When Curt Cobain pulled the trigger on the shotgun he jammed in his mouth, he was recovering after drug and alcohol treatment. When Terri McGovern, daughter of former U.S. Senator George McGovern, died of exposure in a snow bank, she was recovering after drug and alcohol treatment. When his cocaine-ravaged heart could take no more, 50-year-old former all star and World Series MVP Darrell Porter was found dead in a park; he was recovering after drug and alcohol treatment. When he blew his brains out, Hugh O'Connor, son of Carroll O'Connor, was recovering after drug and alcohol treatment. When years of substance abuse finally killed Jerry Garcia, he was receiving, yet again, drug and alcohol treatment. When Andy Gibb drank and drugged himself to death, he was recovering after drug and alcohol treatment. When Chris Farley drank and drugged himself to death, he too was recovering.

All are gone. Addictions kill—so it seems.

Trick or treatment. The best-kept secret of America's addiction treatment industry is that it tricks much more that it treats. While their public relations pitchmen paint rosy pictures as they showcase a few newly sober or high profile celebrities, causalities such as those above, and countless others, continue to pile up. They are not simply victims of addictions. They are the sacrificial lambs of an addiction treatment industry (ATI) that boasts, "Treatment works!"

Addiction treatment initiates you into the precarious world of recovery—and recovery programs are everywhere. Booze, other drugs, gambling, food, sex, love, computers. If you can abuse it, there's a program to deal with it. The trouble begins when your abuse develops into addiction. That trouble is magnified when your addiction is labeled a disease. Confusion sets in when the "treatment" for your "disease" requires lifetime membership in quasi-religious societies disguised as recovery programs.

If this sounds strange to you, you're not alone. Such "treatment" benefits only a select few, a fact which has become very obvious. This religious "treatment" is no longer acceptable as the universal remedy for compulsive behavior and addiction. What benefits *you* is the point! You're better off without addictions *and* without "recovery." You can achieve freedom from both. Begin your liberation now by learning what went wrong—and how you can make it right.

The Sacred Cow

Recovery from compulsive behaviors and addictions has become synonymous with the 12-step program of Alcoholics Anonymous. Like aspirin, the steps are prescribed routinely. Worse, despite overwhelming research evidence to the contrary, 12-step programs are prescribed as the only things that work: "Take the steps and call your sponsor. If that doesn't help, you may change your sponsor, but you must take the steps because the steps are the only thing that works." But they don't work for everyone. Far from it. But that matters not at all to 12-step promoters, especially those in the addiction treatment industry.

Twelve-step advocates, especially AA members, interpret the slightest doubts about The Program as personal affronts and condemnation of their beliefs. Martin E.P. Seligman, Ph.D., Kogod Professor and Director of Clinical Training in Psychology at the University of Pennsylvania, confirms this in his book, *What You Can Change and What You Can't:*

> AA does not welcome scientific scrutiny . . . AA is a sacred cow. Criticism of it is rare, and testimonial praise is almost universal. The organization has been known to go after its most trenchant critics as if they were heretics, so criticism, even in the scientific literature, is timid.

A large majority of addiction therapists/counselors promote AA. Not surprisingly, most are AA members. They interpret their clients' "undisciplined" questioning of The Program as typical alcoholic behavior steeped in egotism, riotous self will and, of course, denial. They are also extremely, reflexively defensive, labeling mere questioning of their methods or motives as "AA bashing." In sum, AA and, especially, its commercial branch, the addiction treatment industry, is an ineffective, self-absorbed, monolithic institution whose members work assiduously to deny addicted people life-saving information and alternative modes of recovery. Of course, many of those who do this have good intentions, but they do it nonetheless.

The Recovery Group Movement (RGM)

The recovery group movement drives America's addiction treatment industry. It's a collective effort of people promoting the "treatment works" mantra—authors, AA members, prominent "recovering" people, and, above all, those who own and work in the treatment industry. Under the guise of treatment, they advance their 12-step agenda as a cure-all. The major flaw with the RGM's one-size-fits-all "treatment" plan, is that it does not work, never has worked, and never will work. It is simply not the panacea the RGM touts it to be. Martin Seligman puts it well:

AA is not for everyone. It is spiritual, even outright religious, and so repels the secular-minded. It demands group adherence, and so repels the nonconformist. It is confessional, and so repels those with a strong sense of privacy. Its goal is total abstinence, not a return to social drinking. It holds alcoholism to be a disease, not a vice or a frailty. One or more of these premises are unacceptable to many alcoholics, and these people will probably drop out.

As for outpatient psychotherapy, *there is no evidence that any form of talking therapy—not psychoanalysis, not supportive therapy, not cognitive therapy—can get you to give up alcohol* . . . Overall, recovery from alcohol abuse, unlike recovery from a compound fracture, does not depend centrally on what kind of inpatient or outpatient treatment you get, or whether you get any treatment at all. (emphasis added)

Why do you think so many people bounce in and out of 12-step programs, or check into rehabs three, four, five times and more? The RGM's stock answers range from disease to denial to "grave mental and emotional disorders" (as AA literature states). Society must realize that these "diagnoses" were invented by AA and accepted as fact by a perverse addiction treatment industry largely made up of AA members. This AA make-believe causes needless suffering and death for countless people who innocently present themselves for addiction treatment.

Self-Recovery

What the recovery group movement won't tell you is that the vast majority of people who overcome addictions (that is, actually get over addictions, rather than remain stuck "in recovery" forever) do so without treatment and without participation in AA. Consider the following from the Harvard Medical School's *Mental Health Letter*, August/September 1996:

> *Most recovery from alcoholism is not the result of treatment.* Only 20% of alcohol abusers are ever treated . . . Alcohol addicts, like heroin addicts, have a tendency to mature out of their addiction . . .
>
> In [a] group of self-treated alcoholics, more than half said that they had simply thought it over and decided that alcohol was bad for them. A[nother group] said health problems and frightening experiences such as accidents and blackouts persuaded them to quit...Others have recovered by changing their circumstances with the help of a new job or a new love or under the threat of a legal crisis or the breakup of a family. (Italics added)

And study results from highly respected addiction researchers, Doctors Linda and Mark Sobell, confirm Harvard's 20 %-treatment statistic:

> [S]urveys found that over 77 percent of those who had overcome an alcohol problem had done so without treatment. In an earlier study . . . a sizable majority of alcohol abusers, 82 percent, recovered on their own.

Yet doctors, employers, ministers, family and friends automatically recommend 12-step programs as the road to recovery. Under the umbrella of addiction treatment our courts mandate addicted criminals to rehab/AA in lieu of prison. Addicted prison inmates are denied parole and/or privileges unless they attend AA. Employee assistance programs order AA participation under threat of job loss. Driving privileges remain revoked unless a convicted drunk driver attends AA. Professional licenses are suspended if addicted lawyers or doctors do not attend AA.

If you have any type of "addiction" problem, you must be in a 12-step program, they insist. But should you find The Program ineffective, or question it in any way, you're branded a dissenter, a malcontent in obvious denial who is playing God and is not serious about wanting recovery unless it's on your own ego-inflated terms. Should you relapse, it's back to square one—step 1.

So, what's the upshot of all this? If you have (or even have had) some type of addiction or abuse problem, the unequivocal conclusion of addiction specialists and the entire 12-step community is that there must be something terribly wrong with you. You are placed, or must place yourself, back into the recovery process again and again and again. Rarely is it suggested that The Program offered is simply not beneficial to you. Still more rare is information on the high incidence of self-recovery and the "secret" to accomplishing it.

Instead, you are found guilty of not responding to a spiritual program that is wrongly yet reverently viewed as the cure-all for every addiction. While the old saying, "If at first you don't succeed try, try again" is viable in some circumstances, there comes a time for reflection—a time to stop beating a dead horse and realistically question and reevaluate your methods and motives.

Your life might depend on it. While it's too late to ask Chris, Jerry, Curt, Andy, Hugh, Brynn, Darrell, Phil, or Terri, it's not too late for you. So run—run away as far as possible and as fast as you can from *anyone* who tells you that Alcoholics Anonymous and its 12-step program is the only road to recovery or the best way to recover.

Just Ask Joan

Jumping in and out of 12-step programs, enduring multiple rehab stints, months of addiction counseling, therapy, relapse prevention, and aftercare programs, along with meetings on top of meetings, are all part of a phenomenon I have termed the *recovery merry-go-round*. Only it's not merry and it's often more exasperating than the roller coaster of addiction. The reality is that people caught in the downward spiral of addictive behavior are not recovering, no matter how many times they go through a misguided treatment process, which ritually incorporates a 12-step agenda. Just ask Joan Kennedy—if you can catch her in-between rehab treatments (13 by last count).

It's clear: 12-step based treatment and recovery programs are not the universal answer to overcoming addiction. Yet, time after time people like Mrs. Kennedy are recycled through a twisted process that fails much more than it succeeds. Besides the Mrs. Kennedys, of the 20% who are "treated," it's the Chris Farleys, Brynn Hartmans, and Curt Cobains that we constantly hear about. Even counselors and therapists who are not ardent 12-step supporters jump on the ATI bandwagon, and will "treat" you, for years on end, with the latest in recovery psychobabble. This is the insanity of the recovery group movement and the addiction treatment industry. And it is only a portion of the devastation wrought by the recovery merry-go-round.

There Are Ways

Alcoholics Anonymous first published its tenets in 1939, when its membership numbered approximately 100. Influenced by the Great Depression and Prohibition, Demon Rum was the enemy and who better to stave off a demon than God? God and spiritual matters still play an important role for many in recovery. (Yet, it seems distinctly unspiritual to coerce others to embrace one's own spiritual/religious beliefs, as routinely happens in the U.S. via coerced AA participation.) The Big Book (AA's bible, officially titled *Alcoholics Anonymous*) states:

> The distinguished American psychologist, William James, in his book, *Varieties of Religious Experience*, indicates a multitude of ways in which men have discovered God. We have no desire to convince anyone that there is only one way by which faith can be acquired.

As seen in AA's own basic text, AA didn't expect all alcoholics who desired such an experience to find it through their message. Yet, today, that is exactly what they are supposed to do.

What's more, people do drop out, or fail at working 12-step programs. When this occurs do we conclude that the "demon" has won? That the demon has defeated one's Higher Power? That God has failed? (AA members refer to God as their Higher Power.) Of course not. The person has failed. He's failed to let God remove character defects and is admonished to surrender his life and will to a God of his own conception in preparation for the "miracle" of sobriety. Such teachings are the cornerstone of addiction treatment received behind the closed doors of rehabilitation centers throughout our country, and at virtually every AA meeting.

Then how is it that others achieve sobriety and find happiness outside of the rooms of Alcoholics Anonymous and AA's commercial branch, the rehab centers? Could it be that we are not as powerless as we have been led to believe? Could it be that those promoting 12-step religiosity under the guise of addiction treatment have taken advantage of addiction, with its compulsions and obsessions, to shamelessly bolster the RGM? It is said that God helps those who help themselves. If true, would God really mind if we found our sobriety through an alternative to the AA Program? Would God try to stop us from saving our own lives?

Success Rates

What constitutes success in AA's recovery program? In the foreword to the second edition of the Big Book they write:

> Of alcoholics who came to AA and really tried, 50% got sober at once and remained that way, 25% sobered up after some relapses, and among the remainder, those who stayed on with AA showed improvement.

In Appendix III, "The Medical View on AA," Dr. G. Kirby Collier, Psychiatrist writes:

> Any therapeutic or philosophic procedure which can prove a recovery rate of 50% to 60% must merit our consideration.

First, please note that these figures are pure assertion. The Big Book offers no evidence whatsoever in support of them. Second, please note that the Big Book carefully qualifies AA's alleged success rate by counting only those who "really tried." And even if you accept these self-serving, unsupported figures, this still means that 25% to 50% of those who "really try" do not achieve success through AA. Should these AA "failures" be conveniently categorized as "in denial," hopeless or unwilling to change?

The Big Book's alleged "success" percentages are over 60 years old and reflect an AA membership that actively sought out The Program. Those figures may have been accurate when enrollment numbered a few dozen, but they are not relevant today. And drop out rates are never mentioned. Instead, AA deals only with those who "really tried."

The only two controlled studies of AA ever conducted both concluded that AA's success rate is no better than the rate of spontaneous remission; that is, those who participated in AA did no better than those who were left totally on their own. Despite that, the RGM boasts of AA's "unparalleled success" based on uncontrolled studies. But AA's own most recent surveys reveal huge dropout rates: 75% after ten meetings, and 95% before one year. Of the 5% who last a year, only 45% reach at least five years sobriety. This means that fewer than three in 100 people entering AA achieve five years sobriety. If AA claims a 3% success rate from its own surveys, it must also take responsibility for its dismal 97% failure rate.

It's also worth noting that the 3% success rate does not refer to those who have stayed continuously booze free. Rather, it refers to continuous membership in AA, which is most definitely not the same thing as continuous abstinence. To paraphrase Ken Ragge (author of *The Real AA*), the only thing more common in AA than abstinence is binge drinking. Because of this, 12-step treatment providers and other AA members regard relapse as a normal part of the "recovery process." And, incredibly, Alcoholics Anonymous is still touted by the RGM as the only thing that works! The sad fact is that AA works very well—for very few.

What about people ordered to attend AA, who would otherwise not be there? Consider the following from the Harvard Medical Schools' *Mental Health Letter*:

> Since assignments to AA are sometimes made by courts, probation officials, and parole boards, a form of controlled research is possible. One study found no long-term difference between problem drinkers assigned at random by a court to Alcoholics Anonymous and a control group assigned to no treatment. Another investigation compared alcoholic heroin addicts who were given methadone alone with addicts assigned to AA and members of another group trained in controlled drinking. Among the patients who completed treatment (fewer than 20%), AA was least effective.

When You Say So

The RGM considers relapse part of the recovery process, and since AA claims glowing success, most members become frustrated when they don't experience "the good stuff," let alone achieve lasting sobriety. They suffer bitter relapses.

This isn't surprising. Twelve-step success implies life in sobriety anchored in faith and spirituality, inspired through one's Higher Power and the wisdom, courage, and serenity that only He can provide. But the belief that 12-step programs will universally awaken these qualities among those who seek such experiences (under the delusion that such experiences are necessary to end an addiction) is simply not credible. It's a fantastic notion fiercely promoted by the RGM as the only way to recover, and the main reason so many unwitting substance abusers trudge in and out of 12-step programs and rehabs year after dreary year. The idea that a group-inspired "spiritual awakening" is the only way to overcome addictions is the only thing taught. This leads many, many people indoctrinated into this belief to anguish, confusion, and hopelessness in the mystical 12-step world of recovery. Like lab rats lost in a maze, they are trapped on the recovery merry-go-round in a futile bid to grab the elusive brass ring of a supernaturally managed sobriety.

So, what then does constitute success for those desiring an end to addiction? No single definition applies to all individuals. However, we do know that quitting an addiction is intensely personal. It is unique to every individual. It is something felt in your bones, not worn on your sleeve. Success does not depend on the accolades and backslapping of group members. It doesn't require cakes or symbolic "chips" marking how good you've been. (Besides, you'll have to turn in your chips as punishment for being bad [relapsing].) Here's the score: It is your progress, your satisfaction, and your happiness that ultimately determines your success or failure in overcoming an addiction. You're a success when *you* say so, not the RGM.

Please understand, "success" is highly subjective. When you succeed, you'll feel it, and those close to you will see encouraging changes in your outlook and behavior. In other words, you are much better off thinking of recovery as being the permanent end of an addiction (yes, you will do this) and living post-addiction life on your own terms (yes, you will do this, too).

There is a distinct difference between quitting your addiction for good and living life after beating an addiction. Calling post-addiction life "recovery" is misleading. In reality "being in recovery" means staying stuck, staying focused on the past, staying focused on what was an unhealthy part of your life—and spending week after week, month after month, year after year, sitting in meeting rooms.

You don't need to do that. There's no reason to endure the RGM's "recovery" process. You can recover permanently without their "help."

Get Ready

The AA "recovery" package includes abandonment of your core beliefs and your self-direction. In AA jargon this is euphemistically referred to as, "letting go of your old ideas absolutely." The purpose is to unlearn self-defeating behaviors, turn your life and will over to a Higher Power, and become one of the one-in-thirty-three AA members who succeed in quitting booze (barring occasional relapses).

But doing the opposite of this, standing on your own two feet and thinking for yourself, will be a powerful force in forging a new life of discovery, not recovery. And by enriching your own life, you'll enrich the lives of others. Whether you are currently in a 12-step program, are contemplating joining one, or feel exploited by the recovery group movement, always remember that you have choices. Right now, you can choose between learning from the real experts on overcoming addiction—the 77 to 82% of the self-discovered who know how to quit, or the "recovering" 3% of AA members who don't.

In the next chapter, you'll discover how the recovery merry-go-round operates. You'll meet "Charlie" and follow his rocky recovery ride. You'll also discover how the disease theory of alcoholism/ addiction fuels recovery mania. So, if you desire freedom from alcohol, drugs and recovery, read on. Get ready to jump off the recovery merry-go-round.

Chapter 2

The Recovery Merry-Go-Round

"Slippers in AA use R.D.P.—Revolving Door Policy"
—AA Slogan

Riders and Operators

The recovery merry-go-round is comprised of two groups: riders and operators. Riders get nowhere fast. These are 12-step members who sense something amiss in their one-day-at-a-time sobriety quest, yet dutifully follow the "recovering" crowd with its hypnotic talk of serenity. Many riders have endured multiple rehab stints. They are RGM pawns who swell the ranks of AA. When not relapsing, they attend meetings, the lifeblood of 12-step programs, like clockwork (in the belief that this will help them avoid relapses). They hold the mistaken belief that 12-step "recovery" is their only hope. Fear of failure, anxiety about maintaining sobriety, and exaggerated notions of personal powerlessness keep them obedient groupers. Round and round on the recovery merry-go-round they spin, always 24 hours away from relapse and ruin. As you will discover, they can free themselves from their recovery ride to nowhere—but most never do, because they've been led to believe that they can't.

Operators keep the merry-go-round spinning. They consist of two sub-groups: 1. Professionals. 2. Innocents

Professionals

Twelve-step "professionals" keep the merry-go-round spinning for two reasons: 1) personal, political, or financial gain; 2) fanaticism. Among them are the addiction counselors and therapists claiming to treat your addiction. These addiction "experts" use new-age psychobabble such as: "acting out," "dealing with your dysfunctional family system," "defining appropriate boundaries," "carrying emotional baggage," "getting in touch with your inner child," "healing your adult-child issues," "identifying your underlying living problems," and "resolving your resentment, anger and relationship issues."

They also want you to stay "in recovery" forever, which is a clue to their incompetence. Most are AA members, and recruiting you gives them personal satisfaction along with a paycheck. These professional operators normally reject recovery alternatives out of hand.

Staunch 12-step members for example, have a personal stake in keeping the merry-go-round turning. It justifies their multiple relapses and rehab stays, because they can blame their disease. For them, it's AA, or no way. And, if they have to work The Program, so do you. They are vocal supporters of the addiction treatment industry, which conveniently supplies them with a steady stream of new members and income (if they're among the many, many AA members who work in that industry). Indeed, addiction treatment for them boils down to: join AA, admit that you are powerless over alcohol, turn your life and will over to a Higher Power and practice the 12-steps.

Some professional operators have financial and/or political motives. Twelve-step recovery is a $10-billion-dollar-a-year industry, and other operators in academia or government agencies need big bucks to keep their programs running and their paychecks coming.

As part of the RGM, The National Council on Alcoholism and Drug Dependence is backing a constituency project called Friends of Recovery (FOR). Based in New Jersey, FOR is an organization committed to promoting 12-step programs through legislative advocacy and by positioning 12-step/AA members in key community positions to influence public policy. Federal and state funding supports the project. Most recently, FOR received a $1 million grant from the federally funded Substance Abuse and Mental Health Services Administration. FOR's lobby has earmarked the money for proselytizing government officials and for organizing events and membership drives. Their vision includes a FOR chapter in every state.

Professional operators have a clear mission: to keep the recovery merry-go-round operating full tilt—for their benefit, at your expense.

Innocents

Innocents are well meaning people who take the slanted advice of the professionals as gospel. They include your neighbors, media personalities, judges, entertainers and other influential public figures who champion addiction treatment based on the half-truths and outright falsehoods spread by the professionals. Beguiled through misinformation and outright lies, innocents believe that "treatment works" and steer addicted family and friends to it. So, by design or default, anyone endorsing addiction treatment as practiced in America keeps the merry-go-round spinning.

Unless noted, future reference to merry-go-round operators does not include the innocents. Their ignorance, though it keeps the merry-go-round turning, precludes them from purposefully doing so. (A good example of one such "innocent" is actor William Shatner. His wife Nerine died of drowning in 1999 while intoxicated, after years of membership in AA and two rehab stints, one at the Betty Ford Clinic. Shatner's reaction? Financial support for Friendly House, a 12-step rehab facility.)

Beyond Unethical

How many times have you heard that "denial" is the barrier to overcoming addiction? Well, denial is alive, well and painfully obvious—in those who claim to treat addictions. To ritually prescribe the same 12-step remedy when symptoms (relapse) regularly reappear or show little improvement is delusional. It makes no sense medically, psychologically, or ethically, especially when there are better options. To continually prescribe the same treatment (for everyone), in the face of near-continual treatment failure, shows denial of the highest order: denial of the obvious, that 12-step treatment is a dismal failure.

It is equally nonsensical and beyond unethical for treatment providers to then fault you for not responding to their ineffective treatment. One strongly suspects that many operators know the truth, but choose to deny it in order to protect their paychecks and their cherished identities (as "recovering" alcoholics or addicts).

Charlie's Rocky Recovery Ride

This is the story of a "recovering" AA member I'll call Charlie. Charlie is actually a composite of three real people who met in rehab: two men, one in his thirties, who is divorced, the other in his forties, married and the father of two, and a single mother in her twenties. All three have ridden the recovery merry-go-round. Their story is the rule, not the exception.

Charlie's a likable guy. He's had some rough times, but then, "Who hasn't?" he'd say to himself. He had a tendency to drink a bit, even over do it now and again. While it was never a major problem, he thought about it often. As time passed, his drinking began to make him lose his edge. Family and friends noticed the change and urged him to seek help, but Charlie refused. He was only wound up a bit, stressed. He'd simply learn to relax more.

Charlie formulated an equation: Alcohol = Relaxation. He didn't realize that for him the equation actually read: Alcohol = Restlessness. As his drinking continued, Charlie became anxious and withdrawn. His health suffered and his self-esteem ran low. He felt uncomfortable and began compromising his values. His job was on the line and friends began drifting away. His family merely tolerated him.

After a drunk driving conviction and hangovers too numerous to count, Charlie came to the conclusion that he was on a dead-end road and needed to stop drinking. Even through his haziness, Charlie felt that quitting for good was his best option. For him, a drink or two would only be a pointless tease. He was reminded of the old potato chip commercial which prodded, "Bet you can't eat just one." If Charlie couldn't have the whole "bag," it was better not to have any.

With his remaining presence of mind, Charlie sought medical advice. The test results were not surprising: high blood pressure, the beginning of a stomach ulcer, liver damage, and irregular heartbeat. Charlie was a physical mess, and his emotional state wasn't much better. He needed to stop drinking, and he asked his doctor for advice. Hospitalization wasn't necessary, so Charlie's doctor dispensed the usual prescription: 90 AA meetings in 90 days, and life-long, regular doses of AA thereafter. Charlie was headed for the merry-go-round ride of his life.

For a short time, all seemed well. Charlie acknowledged his "disease" and sought help. He was taken with The Program and experienced a long-lost enjoyment of life. (A pink cloud, in AA terms, is a false serenity followed by a crash, which can only be alleviated through continued AA involvement.) He dove into The Program, practicing its principles to the best of his God-given abilities in all his affairs. He followed the suggestions, was sincere in his motives, yet struggled terribly.

A few months later, he realized his worst fear: Charlie relapsed. He prayed, he hoped, he questioned, he cried. "Always remember, Charlie, that we're powerless over alcohol and our lives are unmanageable. Surrender! Turn your life and will over to the care of your Higher Power," counseled his AA sponsor.

So, Charlie started back at the beginning, assuming that he'd done something horribly wrong. He blamed himself for failing to grasp AA's "simple program." He dug deeper into The Program, now a daily reminder of his powerlessness and character defects. He no longer trusted his own judgments. Perhaps it was The Program, which must take him. After all, as the Big Book cautions, "At times there is no human defense against the first drink."

Charlie's mind was abuzz. In his head was a haunting echo. An echo sounded by his sponsor and at the beginning of every meeting. An echo so loud he feared for his sanity—the echo of "How It Works" (Chapter 5 of the Big Book, from which passages are read aloud at meetings).

It describes in graphic detail those individuals who do not recover. They are described as constitutionally incapable of being honest with themselves, as unfortunate individuals who through no fault of their own were born that way. The Big Book describes others as suffering from grave emotional and mental disorders. God forbid that he fell into those categories, Charlie told himself. He couldn't be that bad. So, again, he assumed that he must have been doing something very, very wrong. Could it be any other way?

Charlie continued working his program earnestly and in good faith, but demon rum came calling one time too many. A second relapse took a great emotional and physical toll. Charlie was hospitalized. With his medical needs met, including a five-day detox, it was time for the next move: rehab.

Charlie quickly learned that his rehab treatment hinged on the AA program. The Big Book was required reading, meetings were held daily, and the 12-steps were posted on nearly every wall. Now he was convinced that his struggle with sobriety stemmed from his failure to "turn it over" to his Higher Power, although he honestly believed that he had already done so. "It works if you work it," he would hear, so again Charlie dove in with all the faith, hope, and courage he could muster.

After discharge, Charlie worked his program through meetings, action and prayer. He believed and he tried, yet he felt restless; he felt something missing. His sponsor advised, "Just don't drink and go to meetings." "Bring your body and your mind will follow," he preached. "Fake it till you make it," said his aftercare rehab counselor. "Fake it," mused Charlie, "Haven't I been dishonest long enough?" he wondered.

Charlie relapsed again. He returned to his doctor, who prescribed another stretch in rehab. Armed with toothbrush and Big Book, Charlie was shipped off. As before, his medical needs were addressed and private counseling eased his mind as therapy began. The "therapy"? You guessed it: intensive AA indoctrination focusing on his powerlessness, his need to be restored to sanity, and his need to turn his life and will over to the care of God as he understood Him (steps 1, 2 and 3). Again, rehab consisted of 28 days of concentrated introspection, surrender of self, and admission of powerlessness and insanity. Discharge day found a humbled Charlie praying that God's will for him was, finally, peace.

So, the treatment cycle continued and the recovery merry-go-round spun on and on. Meeting after meeting, Charlie found himself more confused than ever. Taking it one day at a time, he prayed. He believed that his Higher Power would restore him to sanity and that his life and will were in His care. But the serenity promised by AA eluded Charlie, and again he thought of the unfortunate people who never recover. Was he one of them?

Charlie's frustrations mounted. While the fellowship provided a sympathetic ear, the "good stuff" he'd heard so much about seemed a distant dream. With his emotional state shot, Charlie looked beyond The Program. He'd gladly have welcomed the slightest glimmer of hope, spiritual or earthly.

Charlie met with his parish priest. "Attend more meetings of Alcoholics Anonymous," the priest counseled. "Every day twice a day if you have to, and remember, our door is always open, too."

He spoke with a psychiatrist who pushed medication and therapy in addition to AA. "The Triple Crown of Recovery," thought Charlie, "Freud, Prozac and God."

He spoke with a neighbor who told Charlie all he knew about overcoming alcoholism. "Join AA and go to their meetings," he parroted, with innocent sincerity. "I know it's the only way to stay off the sauce, because Ann Landers and Dear Abby always send their readers there."

Family members spouted their Al-Anon teachings. (Al-Anon is a fellowship for family and friends of alcoholics, also based on AA's 12 steps.) "Continue with AA," they cautioned. "It's your lifeboat, and without it you'll surely sink."

Charlie called a radio shrink, who urged AA. He spoke with a social worker who advised AA. A telephone hotline counselor, the mailman, a judge, his mother-in-law, a cop, his butcher, his barber—all urged AA, AA, AA, meeting after meeting, rehab after rehab.

Now there was no doubt in Charlie's mind. He must be a recovery failure. As his AA literature described it, he was one of the "poor unfortunates." DOOM!

Suddenly, Charlie got a brilliant idea. He could start all over again; go right back to the beginning and work The Program like no one had worked it before. He could even check into rehab again if his medical insurance would still cover it. Never mind that the "good stuff" and "promises" he'd heard so much about would go unfulfilled, he just wouldn't be all those terrible things his Program attributed to people who do not recover.

"That's it," Charlie reasoned. He'd simply start all over again, go right back to step 1 and figure out what was wrong. Most importantly, he'd start all over and figure out what was wrong with him. As the Big Book says: "Rarely have we seen a person fail who has thoroughly followed our path." Poor, poor Charlie, he was trapped. Trapped in the vicious cycle of the recovery merry-go-round.

It Shouldn't Happen to a Dog

Vince Fox, author of *Addiction, Change and Choice* defines alcoholism as "a phenomenon characterized as physical, mental, and emotional, and treated in medical settings by non-medical personnel with a religious program in which the patient is admitted as diseased, discharged as diseased, permanently recovering, and never recovered."

This is what Charlie was up against when he presented himself for addiction treatment. He was labeled alcoholic, tagged as having the "disease of alcoholism," and kept in perpetual "recovery." Alcoholics Anonymous was thrust upon him no matter where he turned.

Charlie's story illustrates the senselessness of clinging to any program (or enduring any treatment) that is not helping you. Yet, for people like Charlie, admitting that fact is nearly impossible. Counselors, sponsors, and group members all preach the notion of "How It Works" to vulnerable members:

> Rarely have we seen a person fail who has thoroughly followed our path. Those who do not recover are people who cannot or will not completely give themselves to this simple program, usually men and women who are constitutionally incapable of being honest with themselves. There are such unfortunates. They are not at fault; they seem to have been born that way. They are naturally incapable of grasping and developing a manner of living which demands rigorous honesty. Their chances are less than average. There are those, too, who suffer from grave emotional and mental disorders, but many of them do recover if they have the capacity to be honest. (The Big Book)

AA members become as fearful of leaving The Program as they are of booze. They fear AA's ominous predictions about those who fail to work The Program (threats of jails, institutions, or death). They fear their thoughts (referred to as "stinking thinking"). They fear relapse (believed to be a disease symptom). They fear the people, places and things that will "compel" them to engage in addictive behavior (blamed on powerlessness and unmanageability). They fear independent living (identified as life outside The Program).

Because of their fear, cutting the AA umbilical cord proves difficult for many. America's AA-based addiction treatment industry instills this fear and guilt, and this keeps myriads of susceptible people from achieving the happiness and true freedom from addiction and recovery that they deserve.

AA's description of those who fail should have no place in a recovery program that prides itself on "rigorous honesty." Not only does it lead to endless bouts of self-torture, but it is highly unlikely that the 97% of those who try and "fail" at AA all lack honesty. So, it seems that AA's description of those who "fail" is itself dishonest.

Charlie's story highlights another tragedy of the recovery merry-go-round: repeat treatment. While Charlie was willing to try it unreservedly, AA's tonic did not help him in achieving the "spiritual awakening" thought necessary to achieving sobriety. Nonetheless, operators conveniently label all Charlies as poor unfortunates, incapable of honesty, or as being guilty of looking for an "easier, softer way." At best, they might agree with Charlie's decision to start all over again, because, "It works if you work it."

Professional operators, Certified Alcohol Counselors (CAC's) for example, view Charlie's struggles as self-deception. According to them, Charlie demonstrates "self-will run riot," and he only wants recovery on his own "ego-inflated terms." He wants what he wants when he wants it.

If Charlie would go to them again, he'd be counseled to humble himself, whether he thinks he already has or not, and he'd be reminded that his way of doing things results in disaster. They'd tell him that his "best thinking" gets him into trouble, so he'd better surrender, turn himself over to The Program, and admit his powerlessness. (Charlie believed that his worst thinking got him into trouble, but no one seemed to credit this rational insight.) He'd be reminded to draw his strength from the AA group and/or his Higher Power. Additional "counseling" would come in the form of AA slogans and clichés: "Let go and let God"; "Keep it simple, stupid"; "Take the cotton out of your ears and stick it in your mouth"; "Faith without works is dead"; "We are only as sick as our secrets"; "Don't drink, read the Big Book, and go to meetings"; "Willpower = our willingness to use a Higher Power"; "Some of us are sicker than others"; "Your Big Book is your sponsor too"; "Backsliding begins when the knee stops bending"; "Recovery never ends: the disease is alcoholISM, not alcoholWASM!"

In other words, AA is Charlie's salvation. There must be something horribly wrong with him if he doesn't get it. Adding to his confusion is that everything he's been taught is a "suggestion." He is free to "take what he wants and leave the rest." He's only to work The Program to the best of his ability, as no one claims sainthood or "has been able to maintain anything like perfect adherence to these principles." So, in one instance he's counseled to thoroughly follow the AA path, in another he's told that everything is a suggestion, in still another that the only membership requirement is the desire to quit, and finally that those who don't succeed at this "simple program" are "unfortunates" "constitutionally incapable of being honest with themselves."

Charlie had the desire to quit drinking. What he didn't have was ethical and helpful treatment.

Alcoholism as a "Disease"

These four words are the foundation of the recovery group move-ment and its marketing/partnership arm, the addiction treatment industry. The intensely promoted disease model of alcoholism is the basis for treatment: You're diseased for life and therefore need life-long recovery. In 1990, the 12-step front group, National Council on Alcoholism and Drug Dependence (NCADD), and the American Society of Addiction Medicine (ASAM, another 12-step front group) approved the following definition of alcoholism:

> Alcoholism is a primary, chronic disease with genetic, psychosocial, and environmental factors influencing its development and manifes-tations. The disease is often progressive and fatal. It is characterized by continuous or periodic: impaired control over drinking, preoccupation with the drug alcohol, use of alcohol despite adverse consequences, and distortions in thinking, most notably denial.

There is no empirical evidence to support this definition. But even if it were accurate, does subjecting the Charlies of this world to recov-ery merry-go-round lunacy make sense? Are multiple rehab stays, with their myopic focus on surrender to AA and its Higher Power, necessary to reverse an "often progressive and fatal, primary, chron-ic disease with genetic, psychosocial, and environmental factors?" I ask again, what does religious conversion have to do with overcom-ing a "disease"? Think about it.

Ah! There's the rub: the word "think." Disease theorists are con-vinced (and will have you convinced) that your thinking is so impaired that only miracles from Higher Powers will restore your sanity. Charlie's ordeal is evidence of this.

And for that matter, the inclusion of "denial" as part of the NCADD/ASAM definition of alcoholism is telling. It's a Catch-22 proposition: If you admit that you're an alcoholic, you're an alco-holic. If you deny that you're an alcoholic, you're "in denial," strong evidence that you are an alcoholic. Either way you lose.

And you can forget about confronting recovery merry-go-round operators about this irrationality. They won't take you seriously, because everything you say stems from your denial. You lose again.

Treat, Treat, Treat

The ultimate purpose of treatment by 12-stepping "professionals" is to convert you to their religious beliefs. The following Big Book excerpt by psychiatrist, Harry M. Tiebout illustrates this well:

> I now conceive the psychiatrist's job to be the task of breaking down the patient's inner resistance so that which is inside him will flower, as . under the activity of the AA program.

All 12-step treatment programs stress that you are powerless, and have both severe character defects and spiritual deficiencies. Addiction counselors want to focus on your personal troubles and emotional disturbances, which in their view make you drink. But do they really? Is it really necessary to submit to therapy in order to stop drinking? Or is this focus on your supposed defects and disturbances just another way to keep you spinning on the recovery merry-go-round, where resolving your issues will require endless analyzing and intrusive counseling.

As well, rehabilitation centers will rate your success based on overall program compliance, psychosocial functioning, and, most importantly, your acceptance of and submission to the AA program. And all the while no one will teach you how to end your addiction for good. In fact, you'll be told you can't. No one will teach you the "secrets" of the self-recovered. But everyone will treat you, and treat you, and treat you again until, as AA puts it, "[You] will suddenly realize that God is doing for [you] what [you] could not do for [yourself]." "Convert, not cure" is a slogan AA should add to its list. In other words, 12-steppers will treat you until you abandon thinking for yourself, until you abandon self-direction.

Addiction treatment and recovery merry-go-round operators are the snake oil and snake oil salesmen of our time. They sell a treatment for a supposedly incurable disease, when the remedy doesn't work and the "disease" is not a disease. (In reality it's an unhealthy behavior pattern, which you can learn to manage.) And Americans have been buying and buying the treatment industry's snake oil, getting sicker and sicker and sicker, and then buying some more.

You have the power to become and remain securely alcohol and drug free. You have always had the power to do this, just as Dorothy always had the power to return home to Kansas, only she wasn't aware of it.

Be Wildly Successful

When people discover that they can permanently find their way out of addiction, and are given the means to do so, they can be wildly successful. This book sets out the means used by the wildly successful self-recovered. Self-improvement projects, be they spiritual, religious, physical, or psychological, are not necessary to quitting any addiction. To get and stay sober, you and all the self-recovered don't need acupuncture, anger management therapy, aroma therapy, biofeedback, drug and alcohol counseling, exercise programs, group therapy, herbal therapy, inner child healing, light therapy, multidimensional family therapy, multisystemic therapy, past life regression therapy, psychotherapy, relationship therapy, religious conversion, repressed memory therapy, spiritual awakenings, supportive expressive therapy, or therapeutic touch therapy.

Behaviors are not diseases. Alcoholism is behavior that you can stop practicing just as you can stop practicing racism or sexism. You can even stop practicing Catholicism, Judaism or Islam. No one describes people who practice these behaviors as having the diseases of racism or Catholicism, for example. And no one need describe people who practice alcohol dependence as having the disease of alcoholism.

For better or worse, these belief-based behaviors, (like the practice of alcoholism) fulfill a need. But when beliefs change, the need is outgrown, or practicing them becomes detrimental to your health or happiness, you can stop practicing any of them—without treatment and recovery groups.

A case in point is the thousands of Vietnam veterans who addicted themselves to heroin. Studies show that a large majority of them quit their addictions on their own, because: a) their beliefs changed; b) they outgrew the need; c) their health and happiness were threatened.

You are much more than an addiction. The RGM doesn't want you to know that. I do. Identifying yourself as the victim of mythical diseases keeps you spinning on the recovery merry-go-round—forever: "My name is Bob, and I'm an alcoholic," "My name is Brenda, and I'm an addict."

Start empowering yourself now—no matter what your circumstances. Begin now and stop the label game. You don't have to brand yourself a "recovering" anything just because the RGM says so. Never forget that you are always a worthwhile human being much bigger than any addiction.

The next chapter examines the core of 12-step programs: spirituality. It reveals the truth behind AA's spiritual sobriety society. And the truth, as you'll discover, has more to do with advancing the 12-step faith than it has to do with your sobriety, happiness, or spirituality.

Chapter 3

God Help Us: The Trouble with Spirituality

"A man's ethical behavior should be based on sympathy, education and
social ties and needs; no religious basis is necessary."
—Albert Einstein

As part of the recovery group movement, the addiction treatment industry has embraced faith healing as the cornerstone of addiction treatment. The 12-step recovery method hinges on "spiritual awakening," reliance on a power greater than oneself, and spreading the news of this sobriety "miracle" while working with others. The Big Book appendix titled "Spiritual Awakening" states:

> We find than no one need have difficulty with the spirituality of the program. Willingness, honesty and open mindedness are the essentials of recovery.

All the willingness, honesty and open mindedness on earth won't change the fact that most substance abusers find AA's solution unattractive. They also find it ineffective—not only for achieving sobriety, but for becoming "spiritual" as well. In other words, there is much dissatisfaction with AA's formulaic 12-step path to spiritual recovery.

Remember Charlie? Charlie was amenable to a spiritual approach, yet struggled horribly. The fear and guilt associated with not growing along AA's prescribed spiritual lines had him spinning endlessly on the recovery merry-go-round. Charlie was vulnerable, believed AA's promises of spiritual healing as the sole road to sobriety, and he suffered terribly as a result.

The Big Book quotes medical professionals, clergymen and members as endorsing AA's formula for spiritual enlightenment, with the steps being the blueprint for a sober and gratifying life. Indeed, the twelfth step reads:

Having had a spiritual awakening as the result of these steps, we tried to carry this message to alcoholics, and to practice these principles in all our affairs.

The theme is clear: spiritual growth is essential to relieving alcoholism; and a spiritual awakening is your reward for working the steps. So, AA provides the blueprint and merry-go-round operators impose it. Duped by the RGM's relentless promotion of addictive disease as fact, even innocents support it. Alcoholism: the only disease that you are yelled at for having, that can't be cured, and can only be held in check by God.

Here Comes the Judge

The October 14, 1939 *Journal of the American Medical Association* reviewed the Big Book, *Alcoholics Anonymous*, soon after its publication:

The seriousness represented by addiction to alcohol is generally underestimated . . .
For many years the public was beguiled into believing that short courses of enforced abstinence and catharsis in "institutes" and "rest homes" would do the trick, but now . . . a considerable number of other forms of quack treatment have sprung up.
The book under review is a curious combination of organizing propaganda and religious exhortation. It is in no sense a scientific book, although it is introduced by a letter from a physician who claims to know some of the anonymous contributors who have been "cured" of addiction to alcohol and have joined in an organization which would save other addicts by a kind of religious conversion.
The book contains instructions as to how to intrigue the alcoholic addict into acceptance of divine guidance in place of alcohol in terms strongly reminiscent of Dale Carnegie and the adherents of the Buchman ("Oxford") movement. The one valid thing in the book is the recognition of the seriousness of addiction to alcohol. Other than this, the book has no scientific merit or interest.

How a book the AMA called"quack treatment" having "no scientific merit" became the exclusive textbook for treating our addicted masses is astonishing, especially since success rates, as noted earlier, for this type of "treatment" are so abysmal. The reason that this "solution" became the norm in American addictions treatment is that the relatively few people who have found what they believe to be the spiritual solution to alcohol addiction promote it with religious zeal. Many of these individuals have risen to power in the addiction treatment industry. Others hold key government positions. From local intoxicated-driver programs, to state departments of health and human services, to the National Counsel on Alcohol and Drug Dependence, they fervently push their 12-step agenda. They have been very successful in marketing their cause, influencing the medical and legal professions, media, and politicians, and in coercing literally tens of millions of Americans into attending their "humble program of attraction" via the courts, prisons, and employee "assistance" programs.

But there are significant challenges to all this, especially to coercing individuals into 12-step religious indoctrination: In a 1994 federal court case, *O'Connor v. The State of California*, it was ruled that AA is a religious organization and its 12-step program may not be offered in any state-funded or state-administered program without a clear, secular alternative. In 1996, the New York Court of Appeals, in its *Griffin v. Coughlin* decision, found 12-step programs to be "unequivocally religious," and that forced participation in AA was unconstitutional. The Seventh Circuit Court in Wisconsin, in *Kerr v. Farrey*, has also identified AA's 12-step program as "unequivocally religious" and ruled that there must be choice in addiction treatment. In 1997, The Supreme Court of Tennessee found in *Evans v. The Board of Paroles* that AA is "religious," ruling against forced participation of prisoners in Alcoholics Anonymous. There are more cases pending.

Assigning people into spiritual/religious organizations through state or federally funded programs is unconscionable and now increasingly illegal. Coercing susceptible individuals into religious indoctrination under the ruse of addiction treatment should be anathema to the addiction treatment industry. It is beyond unethical. But it is still the norm. There is no binding national precedent banning this practice, because the Supreme Court has not yet heard a case on the matter of AA's religiosity.

Here Comes the Defense

Yet AA partisans fiercely deny that AA is religious. They push their "God as you understand Him," and "Anything can be your Higher Power" stratagems as proof that AA is not conventionally religious, only spiritual. But this doesn't hold water. While it may be unconventional, AA's deity du jour is still that—a deity. AA bases its 12-steps on the belief that only a Higher Power can relieve the compulsion to drink. There is direct reference to a "Higher Power," "God," and "Him" in steps 2, 3, 5, 6, 7, and 11. Prayer is the centerpiece of step 11. The 12th step, spiritual awakening, is your rainbow's-end pot of gold. And there are rituals and sacred readings from the AA "Bible" (The Big Book) at almost all AA meetings. (The only exceptions I can think of are the rare "atheists and agnostics" meetings one very occasionally finds in liberal metropolitan areas.) One also finds evangelism; fearless moral inventories; meditation; prayer; proselytizing; public confession; and candlelight vigils. And as happens at most worship services, AA meetings pause to ritualize their seventh tradition: a collection is taken.

Despite these religious practices, AA refers to its program as "spiritual, not religious." Despite the fact that nowadays a good majority of newcomers are coerced into attendance, AA maintains that its program is "one of attraction, not promotion." This is double talk. While some AA members oppose coercing people into AA, other AA members—including judges, probation officers, and, especially, employee assistance program and treatment facility staffers—enthusiastically take part in the coercion. Even more disturbing is the addiction treatment industry's prescribing of these religious rituals as addiction treatment.[1]

Groupies

There is no reason to believe that belonging to any 12-step program, religion, club, sect, cult, or any other program, will produce the spiritual epiphany that 12-steppers believe is necessary to end addictions. Yet, for many people needlessly trudging through recovery, their "treatment" and AA programming has them wrongly assuming that spirituality can only be awakened by forever working the steps. Like a fly repeatedly slamming into a window, these sorry merry-go-round riders seek freedom where none exists.

---

1. For a thorough discussion of AA's religious nature, see *Resisting 12-Step Coercion: How to Fight Forced Participation in AA, NA, or 12-Step Treatment*, by Stanton Peele, Charles Bufe, and Archie Brodsky. For a discussion of AA's religious roots, see *Alcoholics Anonymous: Cult or Cure?*, second edition, by Charles Bufe, and *The Real AA*, by Ken Ragge.

Indeed, you are taught it is necessary to follow the spiritual teachings of two self-labeled, powerless alcoholics called Bill W. and Dr. Bob, AA's co-founders, Bill Wilson and Robert Smith. That's right, you need to become a Bill W. groupie if you want to escape addiction. (Wilson is considered the key co-founder.) For all of Bill's and Bob's good intentions, mandating their program as essential to addiction treatment is a recipe for failure. Do we mandate Richard Simmons' "Sweatin' To The Oldies" as vital to losing weight? For all Mr. Simmons' good intentions, his program does not benefit everyone— just as AA's program does not benefit everyone. Addicted people should be free to accept or reject Wilson's views just as overweight people are free to accept or reject Simmons' ideas for losing weight. Yet, over one million Americans are coerced into alcohol or drug treatment annually, and approximately 95% of America's rehabs mandate spiritual awakenings through Bill's and Bob's program. Such tyranny is the driving force behind the continuation of our national disgrace: the recovery merry-go-round.

Fun on the Phone

Here's something you can try right now. Look up Alcoholism or Drug Abuse/Addiction in the Yellow Pages. Call a few rehabs and counseling centers. Ask about their programs. You'll hear impressive plans for structuring treatment to your individual needs. Ask if they incorporate the 12-step model. Then ask, if based on your individual need, whether you could receive "treatment" without it. Prepare to hear variations of: "AA's the best thing there is"; "It's helped more alcoholics than anything else"; "Addicts need the support and spiritual path that 12-step programs provide"; "AA's not religious, but members are encouraged to use a Higher Power for guidance."

For more phone fun, call those alcohol and drug abuse hotline numbers found in the front of your directory. Say, "I'm looking for help with alcoholism." Like programmed androids, they will send you to the nearest meeting (groupie gathering) of "recovering" Wilsonites.

Except for the acknowledgment that rehabs encourage clients to use a Higher Power, none of the preceding statements is true. But it doesn't matter that they're not true. What you'll hear from rehabs is the veiled (or sometimes overt) insistence that following Bill Wilson's spiritual program is crucial to overcoming alcoholism and other addictions. In essence, you'll hear that "You must become a Bill W. groupie."

A Spiritual Monopoly

Where is it proven that recovering alcoholics must find their spiritual path, including their conception of a Higher Power (God), through Bill Wilson's philosophy and teachings? It's not in the Big Book. Bill W. and his AA pioneers made it clear that their spiritual recovery plan grew from their own experience, was helpful to them, and then offered it to people who chose to participate. The Big Book states: "Upon therapy for the alcoholic himself, we surely have no monopoly."

Oblivious to this, the recovery group movement and a misled American public have granted a monopoly to 12-step therapy, even after AA's founders admitted its limitations, and that it wasn't for everyone. The proliferation of AA clones is ample evidence of the 12-step influence in American society. Here are but a few 12-step organizations: Al-Anon; Alateen; Cocaine Anonymous; Codependents Anonymous; Emotions Anonymous; Gamblers Anonymous; Incest Survivors Anonymous; Marijuana Anonymous; Narcotics Anonymous; Overeaters Anonymous; Pills Anonymous; Sex Addicts Anonymous; Sex and Love Addicts Anonymous; Sexaholics Anonymous; Workaholics Anonymous.

What these programs have in common is the 12 steps, with only single terms varying in the first and 12th steps, to identify each group's particular concern. This common denominator leaves all participants susceptible to enduring an endless ride on the recovery merry-go-round.

What every 12-step program fails to tell you is that spirituality is a unique and intensely personal experience. It cannot be ordered through the courts or prescribed by faith healers masquerading as professional addiction therapists and counselors. There are many paths to spiritual renewal, if that is what you seek. Explore your options. Read. Talk to people you admire outside the "recovering" world. Don't limit yourself to the RGM's prejudiced view that membership in Bill's and Bob's spiritual awakening club is the only way. It is not! What is touted as spiritual nirvana by the RGM is in reality cultist allegiance to its sainted founder, Bill Wilson, and his stumbling block to sobriety, the 12-step program. So again, *run*, run away as far as possible and as fast as you can, from *anyone* who tells you that Alcoholics Anonymous is the only road to a spiritually satisfying and sober life.

Behold the Steps

In his alcoholic despair, Bill Wilson sought a remedy for his "hopeless" condition. Through a friend, Ebby Thatcher, Bill was introduced to a popular evangelical movement known as The Oxford Groups, or Buchmanism, named after its founder Frank Buchman (1878–1961), a Lutheran minister born in Pennsburg, Pennsylvania. Buchmanism sought to revive the churches through putting its followers in conscious contact with god, thereby providing them (and by extension, their churches) with a spiritual awakening. Anyone familiar with the AA program will recognize the religious/spiritual principles that Buchman promoted: seeking divine guidance; absolute honesty, purity, love, and unselfishness; admission of powerlessness coupled with the belief that humans cannot solve their own problems and need God's help to do so; public and private confession; informality; antipathy toward formal organization; making amends for past wrongs; and sharing of experiences in groups

Bill Wilson and his friends liked Rev. Buchman's philosophy, but they could not fully accept it. They wanted to focus on alcoholism and decided to branch out on their own. (Today, if you don't accept Bill W.'s philosophy, you're labeled a "dry drunk," told you're in denial, possibly sent to jail, denied parole, or lose your job.) Bill and the boys considered Buchman's principles rules, but they didn't easily embrace rules. So, their organization would have none; instead they would have "suggestions." The only membership requirement for Wilson's new group would be a desire to stop drinking. (The type of Higher Power [God] to be relied upon was, supposedly, to be left to members. But Wilson's scriptures clearly reveal what type of Higher Power it really is—a traditional, patriarchal God. See the books mentioned in the footnote on page 27 for in-depth discussions of this matter.) With very minor modifications, Wilson codified Buchman's principles into the 12 steps of Alcoholics Anonymous. Read them, with introduction and closing, as presented in the Big Book:

Remember that we deal with alcohol—cunning, baffling, powerful! Without help it is too much for us. But there is One who has all power—that One is God. May you find Him now!

Half measures availed us nothing. We stood at the turning point. We asked His protection and care with complete abandon. Here are the steps we took, which are suggested as a program of recovery:

1. We admitted we were powerless over alcohol, and that our lives had become unmanageable.
2. Came to believe that a Power greater than ourselves could restore us to sanity.
3. Made a decision to turn our will and our lives over to the care of God, as we understood Him.
4. Made a searching and fearless moral inventory of ourselves.
5. Admitted to God, to ourselves and to another human being, the exact nature of our wrongs.
6. Were entirely ready to have God remove all these defects of character.
7. Humbly asked Him to remove our shortcomings.
8. Made a list of all persons we had harmed and became willing to make amends to them all.
9. Made direct amends to such people wherever possible, except where to do so would injure them or others.
10. Continued to take personal inventory and when we were wrong promptly admitted it.
11. Sought through prayer and meditation to improve our conscious con tact with God as we understood Him, praying only for knowledge of His will for us and the power to carry that out.
12. Having had a spiritual awakening as the result of these steps, we tried to carry this message to alcoholics, and to practice these principles in all our affairs.

Many of us exclaimed, "What an order! I can't go through with it." Do not be discouraged. No one among us has been able to maintain anything like perfect adherence to these principles. We are not saints. The point is, that we are willing to grow along spiritual lines. The principles we have set down are guides to progress. We claim spiritual progress rather than spiritual perfection.

Our description of the alcoholic, the chapter to the agnostic, and our personal adventures before and after make clear three pertinent ideas:

(a) That we were alcoholic and could not manage our own lives.
(b) That probably no human power could have relieved our alcoholism.
(c) That God could and would if He were sought.

Although AA promotes the idea that alcoholism is a disease, note that the 12-Steps do not mention illness or disease; instead they focus on God, self-surrender, moral inventory, atonement, character defects, prayer, and spiritual awakenings. This is directly linked to nineteenth-century Protestant revivalism and is reminiscent of temperance movement piety. You don't have to be an altar boy to realize that praying "for knowledge of His will" (step 11) is essentially "Thy will be done," as invoked in the Lord's Prayer (which, not coincidentally, is said at the end of a good majority of AA meetings). And AA's three pertinent ideas (a, b, c) leave nothing to the imagination regarding the need for a Higher Power to relieve alcoholism. The merits of confession, penance, humility, faith, and honesty exemplify Christian/spiritual living and are 12-step bedrock. Leading a Christian/spiritual life is rewarding for many, but for people who find Bill Wilson's slant on spirituality unhelpful in achieving sobriety, yet have been brainwashed into believing that it's the only way, the step program becomes liability #1.

A Curious Slant Indeed

Bill Wilson claims to have experienced a spiritual epiphany while hospitalized. Under the care of Dr. William T. Silkworth (a Big Book contributor), Wilson was withdrawing from alcohol. The detox treatment used on him was "the belladonna cure": a blend of morphine, belladonna, henbane, and other psychoactive drugs. It was while under the influence of this hallucinogenic "cure" that Bill W. had his "spiritual awakening," in his own words, "a white light experience."

AA's official Wilson biography, *Pass It On*, describes the event in Wilson's own words:

> [I] cried out, "I'll do anything at all . . . If there be a God, let Him show Himself!" Suddenly, my room blazed with an indescribably white light. I was seized with an ecstasy beyond description . . . I was conscious of nothing else for a time . . . I became acutely conscious of of a Presence . . . of living spirit . . . This I thought, must be the great reality. The God of the preachers . . . I thanked my God, who had given me a glimpse of His absolute self.

This glimpse of God was the inspiration for Bill to found AA. It's the same inspiration on which the ATI and RGM base your treatment and recovery.

But Bill Wilson desired greater understanding. Cripplingly depressed throughout his life and at times suicidal, he sought additional ways to expand his consciousness and spirituality. He had a persistent fascination with clairvoyance and other psychic phenomena. He held séances and engaged in conversations with spirits. And while a visit from God was good, it wasn't good enough; he experimented with LSD to heighten his perception and improve his "conscious contact with God." Also, from *Pass It On*, Bill's thoughts on LSD:

> It is a generally acknowledged fact in spiritual development that ego reduction makes the influx of God's grace possible. If, therefore, under LSD we can have temporary reduction . . . well, that might be of some help. . . . So I consider LSD to be of some value to some people, and practically no damage to anyone. . . .
> There is the probability that prayer, fasting, meditation, despair and other conditions that predispose one to classic mystical experiences do have their chemical components. . . . [T]hey do open doors to a wider perception. If one assumes that this is so and there is already some biochemical evidence of it then one cannot be too concerned whether these mystic results are encouraged by fasting or whether they are brought on by [LSD].

Bill Wilson used LSD as a portal to a "wider perception." You don't have to. Nor do you have to accept his spin on spirituality or recovery. Indeed, the next chapter is devoted to discovering your own HP (heightened perception) without psychics, séances, spirits, or LSD.

Like Father, Like Son

The intent of Buchmanism was to revive Christianity through the practices taught by Frank Buchman and his followers. The intent of Alcoholics Anonymous is to revive the spiritual life of the individual through Buchman's practices, as codified by Bill Wilson. Both Wilson and Buchman were fallible human beings. Buchmanism failed to revive Christianity. Alcoholics Anonymous fails to revive the spiritual life in sobriety for everyone seeking it. Bill Wilson's program is not the answer for all people seeking spirituality or trying to end an addiction.

Undeniably, one flawed movement begot another.

They Know Only a Little

Bill Wilson and his early followers knew their limitations. From the Big Book: "Our book is meant to be suggestive only. We realize we know only a little. God will constantly disclose more to you and to us." By its own words, the Big Book leaves the door to spirituality and recovery wide open, because its author admits that he and his followers "know only a little." It is the RGM and its business arm, the addiction treatment industry, that have slammed the spirituality and recovery doors shut.

RGM members shout, "Hey, no one is forced to participate in AA. Everyone is welcome, yet free to leave at any time." Such statements are the epitome of denial. The cost of leaving is often high. Our courts mandate AA attendance, and probation can be revoked or parole denied if one does not "voluntarily" attend AA. Public housing can be denied if a former or current substance abuser does not attend. Life-saving organ transplants can be withheld if it's determined alcohol or illicit drugs caused the illness, and the suffering person refuses to attend AA. Medical and professional licensees can be revoked. Employees can be terminated. While innocent operators and the small percentage of AA members who benefit from The Program perceive this proclaimed sense of freedom as real, it's not a reality for a large majority of merry-go-round riders.

As well, even for those who originally came voluntarily, the indoctrination can prove so powerful that the freedom to leave becomes a freedom in theory only. These riders believe that their lives are unmanageable and that no human power can help them. They suffer crippling relapses while praying to Higher Powers for a miracle. It's no wonder that the sense of freedom so proudly touted by some is nonexistent to merry-go-round riders.

The trouble is not with spirituality. The RGM's insistence that Wilson's program is the only way to achieve it, and that spirituality is necessary to overcoming addictions, is the problem. Also, Wilson's focus on powerlessness and unmanageability fuels learned helplessness: the belief that you cannot help yourself, and that it's pointless to try to do so.

But you can help yourself! What's more, if you overlook the religious vs. spiritual debates surrounding AA, you're still left with a program, (be it religious or spiritual) that fails 97% of the people who try it. That's the reality.

So, how did all this corruption arise? Combinations of religious zeal, denial, willful ignorance, and political and financial gain are responsible for this spiritual-treatment tragedy: the 12-step recovery merry-go-round.

The next chapter will help you rekindle your ability to think for yourself. It goes beyond the disease myth of alcoholism/addiction and Wilson's views on recovery. You'll discover the power you command and begin putting it to work. Let it serve as your own personal awakening. In fact, some of you might find it downright spiritual.

Chapter 4

Heightened Perception: Your Higher, Higher Power

"People are disturbed not by things, but by their view of things."
—Epictetus

"I do not feel obliged to believe that the same God who endowed us with sense, reason and intellect has intended us to forgo their use."
—Galileo Galilei

Wake up! The purpose of this chapter is to jolt you. To knock you out of an RGM-induced haze riddled with false, unproven, and deadly notions of addiction treatment, addictive disease, aftercare, alcoholic and addict labels, codependency, enablers, family disease, group rehabilitation, higher powers, lifelong recovery, 90 meetings in 90 days, powerlessness and unmanageability, relapse prevention programs, spiritual/religious awakenings, and sponsorship.

The truth is that you are not powerless over your desires to use booze, pills, or powders. While you may have behaved powerlessly, the initial choice to drink/use was always yours. You may have agonized over your choice, or you may have acted impulsively, but at no time did an addictive disease hijack your mind and body and force you to drink or use. It can be comforting to believe that you're "powerless," the victim of a "disease" or "cunning, baffling, powerful" substances. But it simply isn't true.

AA members find solace in the disease concept, because it absolves them of all responsibility for past drunken escapades. And because they are never expected to actually quit, just to put it off one day at a time, and to "keep coming back"; future escapades are also pardoned (although errant members are held accountable and will suffer a major loss of status, that is, a loss of "time"). Remember, AA members are not expected, let alone required, to stop drinking; a desire to quit is all that is required of them.

These powerless AA members are one-day-at-a-time time bombs, forever walking on eggshells, desperately afraid that they'll again fall victim to their "disease." Year in year out they attend meetings and call sponsors in an attempt to avoid something that they are taught is beyond all human power to control. Given the desperate, near-hopeless nature of this quest, it's not surprising that so few of them succeed in quitting.

Anything But You

If overcoming the desire to drink is beyond human ability, and, as AA teaches, the group itself can be your Higher Power, does the group possess the spiritual powers AA says are necessary to staying sober? AA seems thinks to think so. This belief is expressed in the creepy, self-referential acronym, "G.O.D., Group Of Drunks." The belief that AA members have superior spiritual development is also found in the common talk at meetings about being "better than well" (than less spiritually developed, regular folks who never had drinking problems).

Besides the group, AA claims that anything can be your Higher Power. Anything except yourself. Self-empowerment is taboo. Your "stinkin' thinkin'," which is an AA cliché applied to those who can still think for themselves, is the culprit. That's why in step 2, Bill Wilson states that only a power greater than yourself can restore you to sanity. After all, you're diseased, powerless, and cannot manage your own life. You must find a Higher Power—but where? How?

Do you own a pet? Do you love nature? Do the oceans or the heavens fill you with awe? Do you have children? Are you lost without your car, computer or cell phone? Pick one. Pick anything for that matter. As long as you're willing to relinquish power to it, to abandon self-direction, you've found step 2's Power greater than yourself. But don't forget, in step 3 you'll be turning your life and will over to that Higher Power—even if it's Rover! And in step 5, you'll admit to Rover the exact nature of your wrongs. In step 6, you'll ask Rover to remove all your character defects. In step 7, you'll ask Rover to remove your shortcomings. And in step 11, you'll pray to improve your conscious contact with Rover, praying only for the knowledge of Rover's will. That Rover must be one special little doggie.

Quitting alcohol and other drugs boils down to the classic moral dilemma: choosing right or wrong, for you. Knowing your own addiction history, is it right or wrong for you to continue on your present course of unpredictable sousing? None of Wilson's steps answer this basic question. If drinking's wrong, then you'll need to discover how to quit, stay quit, and stick with that decision. If it's right, then you're not ready to quit.

It's that simple. But slick rehab programs will have you agonizing over irrelevant spiritual/religious ideas. Therapists will have you probing childhood days searching for the wounded inner child and the trauma(s), which, in their view, fuel your desire to get loaded. It seems everyone is hell bent on "treating" you, for years on end, with impertinent guidance on how to live, who to associate with, where to go, and what to believe.

Sober Yet Drunk?

People immersed in 12-step recovery share needless, yet common frustrations. Confused and unfulfilled, they dutifully "work the program," often for year after frustrating year. Meeting after meeting, they search for the peace and sobriety they believe awaits them. But, for most, peace and sobriety never come, no matter how hard they try. (Remember Charlie?) Eventually some inner voice questions AA's "program" and "the AA lifestyle." Group members, sponsors, and CACs (Certified Alcohol Counselors) view such "difficult" people as "thinking alcoholically," or "seeking a quick recovery fix."

They also attach denigrating labels to those who question the sacred Program. Perhaps most insulting is "dry drunk," an expression coined by the RGM to describe anyone who seems noncompliant or dares deviate from Program norms. They say that failure to "work a good program" spurs the dry drunk syndrome. Yet, of course, there is no cut and dry definition of this term—just being grumpy one day is enough to tag you a dry drunk.

The addiction treatment industry tries to validate AA's dry drunk label. Addiction researchers cite early sobriety anxiety and the tension associated with newly sober responsibilities as the source. Some posit a physiological basis. No matter what the cause, and no matter what the definition, joining AA is still the remedy. In other words, the recovery group movement's pseudo-scientific dry drunk syndrome is remedied with Bill Wilson's pseudo-religious steps.

When members' concerns are addressed, they are met with a hodgepodge of pop psychology, slogans, clichés, or feeble religious incantations. "Let go and let God" is one example. "Utilize, don't analyze" is another. "Don't drink, read the Big Book and go to meetings," pretty much sums it up.

But Alcoholics Anonymous is supposed to be a self-help organization. If it's not helping you, then get out. You'll do much better without all the "Bill-babble" and psychobabble. But the momentum of the recovery merry-go-round often makes such a decision inconceivable. Let's change that.

The Frustration Factor

Frustration is an emotional wake-up call. It's a call to action telling you that things can be better. It's telling you to explore your options. Frustration tells you to examine what you've been taught and how you "see" things. But frustrated people often do none of these things. Instead, many, many people needlessly endure frustration, often for years on end. As a result, they often become less flexible, less imaginative, and certainly less constructive. In short, these people stay stuck. If this sounds like many of the people you meet in AA, it's no accident.

If you don't want to be one of them, your job is to nip frustration in the bud. If you feel you can do better, and what you are doing isn't working, that means you're experiencing frustration. It's time to change your approach. This is not a bad thing; it's a sign of clear thinking. While AA wants you to believe that "your best thinking got you here," don't buy it. Simply by reading this book, you've chosen to think for yourself and to explore your options.

So, think about your own progress toward recovery. Is what you're doing working or not working? Are you experiencing frustration? Read Dr. Wayne Dyer's comments:

> Progress, yours personally and the world's depends on unreasonable men, rather than people who adapt to their society and accept whatever comes along. Progress depends on individuals who are innovators, who reject convention and fashion their own worlds. In order to shift from coping to doing, you'll have to learn to resist enculturation and the many pressures to conform. You may be viewed by some as insubordinate, which is the price you'll have to pay for thinking for yourself. Some people will not take kindly to your resistance to norms they've adopted for themselves.

Many of us would like to give the individual more freedom, freedom from meaningless musts and silly shoulds. What we are striving for is choice, that is, the ability to be free from the servant mentality of constant adherence to the shoulds.

George Bernard Shaw put it this way:

Reasonable people adapt themselves to the world. Unreasonable people attempt to adapt the world to themselves. All progress, therefore, depends on unreasonable people.

And Einstein simply said:

The important thing is to not stop questioning.

By exploring recovery options, you're exercising freedom of choice —freedom to reject the blind obedience expected of you by merry-go-round operators, freedom to reject convention, the pressure to conform; you're asserting your right to question and take an active role in a recovery that makes sense and is right for you. Yes, the RGM "will not take kindly to your resistance to norms they have adopted for themselves." Too bad!

It's clear: Self-efficacy and thinking for yourself terrifies the anti-choice extremists of the RGM. The RGM relentlessly promotes and attempts to impose its vision of "recovery" on everyone. But a closer look reveals what its vision masks—a merry-go-round of frustrated souls desperately seeking an end to their recovery nightmare.

Understanding some of the sad realities of the recovery merry-go-round has, I hope, helped you to see things differently. Call it your HP—your heightened perception. Unlike made-up Higher Powers, heightened perception is your ability to read between the lines, to begin thinking for yourself again, and to make choices. Heightened perception is your "ability to be free from the servant mentality of constant adherence" to the RGM.

Your Higher, Higher Power

How you perceive things means the difference between freedom and imprisonment. Here's one example of how this works: A woman saw herself as defective when she began gaining weight. Diets and exercise helped, but her "defect" persisted. She was uncomfortable in her own skin, leaving her a reclusive spectator in life. Another woman saw herself as a person with a few pounds to lose, not as "defective." Diets and exercise helped, and she lived happily, enjoying life, facing its challenges, and savoring its rewards. When people perceive themselves as defective, whether it is from substance abuse, alcoholism, or being overweight, they feel disempowered and behave as if they *were* defective.

Recovery programs train you to perceive yourself as diseased and as susceptible to relapse at any time. This can be termed "lowered perception." It is the perception of those who consider themselves as being "in recovery"—permanently. They think, feel, and behave as if they are diseased, and they want *you* to think, feel, and behave the same way as they do. That's why I urge you to heighten your perception.

Heightened perception is your higher, higher power. It consists of being conscious, aware, questioning, and thinking for yourself, regardless of the opinions of others. Heightened perception allows you to make your own decisions—especially about how to overcome your addiction.

The Feelings Trap

It's natural that the early days of sobriety are confusing. But this does not mean that you need to spill your guts in rehabs or AA meetings, where addiction counselors would have you expressing feelings and disclosing potentially damaging information non-stop. Learning to deal constructively with your emotions is important, but that is not what you'll learn to do as a vulnerable newcomer in the RGM. In the name of "working the program," they'll have you divulging hurtful and/or irrelevant personal information relating to family, sex, and illegal activities; and this information may come back to haunt you. "Anonymous" does not mean confidential. Information given in meetings, whether in church basements, rehabs, or behind prison walls, can and does leak out. And none of this "work" has anything do to with the matter at hand: ending your addiction.

"Working the program" doesn't teach you that your feelings are products of your own thinking. Precious months or years are wasted on such inanities as whether you see the glass as half full or half empty. Whatever your view, and whatever your feelings, your feelings are given short shrift because your "best thinking" got you where you are: a drunk in AA.

Another reason not to buy into the RGM's emphasis on emotional disclosure at meetings is that the majority of people who quit, especially those who quit outside the influence of the RGM, find that their emotional stability returns in good stead and they begin thinking more clearly in reasonably short order after they quit. Private counseling, in an attempt to catch-up on the "lost" emotional years, is often suggested, but this is nothing more than ATI hype to keep you coming back—especially if you're dealing with a 12-step therapist. For business, political, proselytizing, and identity-maintenance reasons, these counselors need you much more than you need them.

It often takes some time and practice to fully appreciate this, but if you understand that you feel the way you think, you hold a very powerful tool for dealing with the transition from impaired drinker to healthy former drinker. The quotation at the beginning of this chapter states: "People are disturbed not by things, but by their view of things." This is very true, and a very powerful insight. Begin cultivating your heightened perception to better manage your thinking, and hence to improve your emotional state. Change your thinking, and you change your feelings. This prepares you to face any challenge and to act in your own best interest.

For example, should your company "downsize," cries of "What will we do?" fill the air. Many slated for layoff perceive their upcoming firings as something devastating. They feel abandoned and fearful, because they think of this as disastrous. The person with heightened perception isn't happy about this (looking for work is a pain) but he knows his value and he knows his worth. He perceives his situation as a temporary setback; he doesn't think of it as disastrous. While his co-workers feel desperation, the perceptive person feels concern, and is in much better emotional shape to seek out alternatives—alternatives that he or she knows exist.

It can be that easy—you simply need to focus on what you're telling yourself to see that your destructive self-messages are the primary cause of your emotional upset; but you need to practice this effective cognitive technique. The more you do it, the easier it becomes, and it frees you from the RGM feelings trap. Getting mixed up with the RGM in an attempt to break an addiction breeds more dependency—on the RGM. (Wasn't overcoming dependency your original concern?) As you expose yourself to 12-stepping addiction counselors and RGM members, stifling emotional traps can cloud your perception, leading to years on the recovery merry-go-round.

Remember, when you first quit an addiction you're vulnerable, and recovery group members and the treatment industry will go to great lengths to keep you that way. Their goal is to convert you to their 12-step religion. A good step away from this trap is realize that you are not a victim of your emotions, that you are not "powerless" over them. Simply put, to change your feelings/emotions, change your thinking. It works. And it works better and better with practice.

The RGM promotes the idiotic, unsupported idea that an alcoholic's emotional maturity level is what it was when he or she began their drinking career. Adults are routinely told that their emotional level is that of a 15 year old, if that was the age when they began drinking. While this sounds good to treatment professionals, it is simply not true. In fact, it is very harmful to those who buy it, because it keeps them dependent on the "experts" on emotional maturity—AA elders and treatment professionals. But this belief is very helpful to another group—the very same therapists and other treatment professionals who promote this belief. It provides them with a steady stream of paying patients (customers) whose "lack of maturity" and underlying issues need to be flushed out, analyzed, and resolved, sometimes over the course of years.

Nothing More Than Feelings

Rehab group therapy sessions regularly begin by asking members how they are feeling. Words such as "fine," "OK," "good" or "bad" are not acceptable. They are considered superficial, and as masking "true" emotions. To help tell you how you are feeling, many rehabs employ the use of a "feelings wheel." This is a pizza-sized pie chart, which is divided into dozens of slices, each representing a feeling. Anxious members huddle around the chart before upcoming meetings, desperately searching for an acceptable adjective to describe their feelings. They pick one in random panic to avoid the forbidden "fine," "OK," "good," or "bad." In avoiding these generic terms, they also avoid, for the moment, intrusive probing of their "distorted alcoholic minds" by RGM-trained group leaders or CACs, whose basic claim to being counseling professionals is that they are true-believing members of AA or NA.

Crises often draw susceptible people into the recovery group movement. Once drawn in, people never hear about alternatives. All that they ever hear is that the 12-step program is their only hope. And they often eventually end up accepting this, even if they don't want to. How can those of us who have been indoctrinated by the RGM break out of this trap? How can we heighten our perceptions and change our thinking and feelings?

It's hard to do this, because we all have the horrible suspicion that they might be right. We all know of someone who claims success through AA, and we've heard its praises sung for decades. What if the RGM is right?

Let's develop some heightened perception and put to rest any nagging thoughts regarding the merits of AA and the RGM.

Heightened Perception in Action

The 12-step-promoted perception is this: Without AA, your options are jails, institutions or death. Only a Program-inspired Higher Power can restore you to sanity and relieve your alcoholism. You must join other powerless alcoholics in the hope that your group effort will keep you away from demon rum and on the spiritual path of recovery.

The truth is this: The recovery group movement is the result of a man-made program designed and formulated by two men, Bill Wilson and Dr. Bob Smith, for their personal use in a quest for sobriety. In the name of God and spiritual renewal, they offered their suggested program of recovery to "powerless alcoholics." Simply stated, they began AA to help themselves and other people who chose to use their brand of spiritual healing.

Bill and Bob got together in the 1930s when they were both members of the evangelistic Oxford Group Movement (OGM). They borrowed its "program" wholesale, changed some of its terminology, and, after years of operating as part of the OGM, christened the result Alcoholics Anonymous. There is no evidence—absolutely none—that it came about through "divine inspiration." AA is entirely man made.

Saying that you're not helped by participating in AA is nothing more than saying that a man-made program, devised by a couple of self-labeled powerless alcoholics, is not benefitting you. No more and no less. This is not a horrible thing to say. If it's true for you, be "rigorously honest" and say it.

AA's co-founders hinged their recovery program on spiritual growth. The intent is that members develop direct conscious contact with a power greater than themselves, that is, God. This might be inspiring for those amenable to a spiritual approach, but those who are not find themselves frustrated square pegs desperately trying to fit into a round hole. The suffering this has caused since AA came into being is incalculable.

Members who genuinely try, yet struggle or relapse, often conclude that they are failing to achieve conscious contact with God. Even though they've turned their lives and wills over to His care, as step 3 teaches, success and serenity remain a distant dream. Sadly, some begin thinking that while they need a Higher Power, they can't reach it (because they're in some way defective) so it can't help them. No one in AA, with the desire to quit, wants to believe such things about themselves. So they cling to The Program, "work it" desperately, and remain on the merry-go-round regardless of their lack of progress. Anything less would be admitting that they lack the necessary spirituality and are not connecting with their Higher Power. This nonperceptive thinking permeates the recovery merry-go-round and ruins potentially happy, productive lives—lives stolen not only by addiction, but by the recovery group movement.

For those who still feel this way, and are suffering as a result, the heightened perception is this: the only thing you are not connecting with is the teachings of two self-anointed, spiritually obsessed, alcohol-addicted men who took an evangelistic indoctrination program and sold it as a program of "recovery." They did this by themselves, for their own benefit.

God did not write AA's stepping-to-spirituality program. He didn't inscribe the 12-steps on stone tablets and hand them down from some mountaintop. Bill Wilson simply took the Oxford Group Movement's ideology and practices, softened its terminology, and concocted a God-as-you-conceive-Him stratagem so that everyone could join his serenity-seeking club.

There is nothing anti-spiritual, blasphemous or criminal in questioning the value of any program, or the motives of its promoters. If you are involved with AA and the recovery group movement of your own free will, and are happily where you want to be in the Wilsonian world of the perpetually recovering, please consider giving this book to someone less fortunate.

You're On Your Way

The above is an example of how heightened perception can drastically change your thinking and feelings. In this instance, our heightened perception tells us that well meaning yet misguided devotion to Bill W.'s borrowed evangelical program is not in everyone's best interest. The recovery group movement's insidious purpose is to persuade you that the 12-step approach *is* in everyone's best interest, and that only misfits or malcontents question the RGM's methods and motives.

I hope that you understand the power you have to see through such propaganda. A change of perception can unlock doors you never realized existed. Whether your heightened perception comes through science, religion, or reading a book, whether you call it a, spiritual awakening, psychic change, enlightened self-interest, or simply a new attitude, if it makes sense for you, you're on your way. Couple this with a new awareness of the rewards ending an addiction brings, and there'll be no stopping you.

"Every time I think it's time to move on with my life, a whole new set of problems seem to arise." This bleak observation is a common lament by persons in and out of recovery programs. Yet, all too frequently we see the same faces, at the same meetings, bemoaning the same problems and the same frustrations.

Let's amend the quote: "Every time I clear up my problems and think it's time to move on with my life, a whole new set of problems seem to arise. Until one day it dawned on me, this is my life." Now we've hit on something. This is your life and you're free to live it.

The next chapter gives you the opportunity to exercise your newfound heightened perception. You'll spot the tricks of the recovery trade and discover how to counter them. You'll meet "Wayne," who after 16 grueling years has stepped off the recovery merry-go-round. You'll also learn why RGM operators ignore, suppress, or disavow new and lifesaving information, no matter how beneficial, about overcoming booze and other drugs.

Chapter 5

Their Truth and Nothing But Their Truth

"It isn't a mistake to have strong views. The
mistake is to have nothing else."
—Anthony Weston

Stop and think—the entire recovery group movement has a stake
in proving to the world, and above all to itself, that everything they
believe is The Truth. This "Truth" is built upon the fragile foundation
of Bill Wilson's sacred teachings. It provides the RGM with its very
reason for being. With it, RGM members are somebody special
(somebody not only in "conscious contact" with God, but somebody
with sponsors, pigeons, a fellowship, clubhouses, and insiders' 12-
step recovery jargon); without it, they're nobody.

Because the foundation on which AA's Truth sits is so weak, it is
fiercely defended. Any deviation from Wilson's teachings shakes this
foundation to its core. Any questioning of AA's sacred dogma rocks
their world. Unless you accept their Truth, they dismiss you as sick,
in denial, or one of the poor unfortunates. There must be something
inextricably wrong with *you*. And given the RGM's beguilement of
the American public, just about everyone else will think that something is wrong with you, too. (Of course, this *ad hominem* approach
makes it very easy for the RGM's operators to avoid answering questions.)

This book will help to change that.

1984

Alcoholics Anonymous flaunts the virtue of rigorous honesty. It is
supposedly a staple of "the AA way of life." Yet, truth and honesty
are curiously absent when AA's sacred beliefs are questioned. Why?

Because truth and honesty are incompatible with AA's "program," in that they cannot give "recovering" folks what they supposedly need.

And they "need" a great deal. They need to believe in The Program. They need to believe in Bill Wilson, his "divinely inspired" teachings, the 12-step fellowship, and the "wisdom" of Program-savvy sponsors. They need to believe in unmanageable lives, make-believe diseases, and personal powerlessness. Above all, they need to believe in the one-day-at-a-time protection of The Program's super-natural forces: a Higher Power. This Higher Power is supposedly of their own choice, but AA's sacred scripture is written in such a way that it can only be a traditional, patriarchal god. Could you turn your life and will over to a tree, for example, when The Program's third step has you abandoning yourself to your Higher Power? Could you then pray for conscious contact with your "godly" sycamore and beseech the sycamore for guidance?

The real truth is that 12-step sacred beliefs are nothing more than the opinions and spiritual teachings of AA's guru, Bill Wilson. Here's how it works: merry-go-round operators present Bill Wilson's Program as The Truth. They are the enlightened ones who bestow this Truth on "hopeless" alcoholics and addicts. They are the Orwellian masters of irreproachable thought. Their beliefs are as obviously, undeniably true as that the sky is blue. Any information, idea, or question that doesn't buttress The Truth is a threat that must be smothered. And by virtue of their captured audiences, rehab centers are ideally suited for implanting The Truth into the needy.

Isolation and Information Control

The Truth is force fed in a variety of ways. Inpatient rehabs have the advantage of a prolonged indoctrination period in a highly con-trolled environment. "Needy" inductees (patients) are kept in lengthy isolation where information is tightly controlled. They are force fed a steady diet of Wilson's doctrine, and they study his Big Book. Steps 1, 2 and 3 are the focus: powerlessness and unmanage-ability, insanity and surrender. The 24-hours-a-day book provides daily meditations and RGM-approved prayers. Leisure reading material must also be RGM approved. Television and radio pro-grams, mail, computer, and telephone use are strictly controlled or prohibited altogether, and all contact with the outside world is rigor-ously monitored.

Visitors often endure a mini-indoctrination of RGM-approved recovery videos. Rehab personnel (AA recruiters) lecture on the insidiousness of alcoholism and addictive disease. It is only then that many families first learn of their loved one's supposedly incurable progressive disease, and how they too are afflicted with the disease of codependency. Al-Anon—another keeper of The Truth—is their prescribed remedy.

Wayne

One such "needy incurable" is "Wayne." Wayne was on the recovery merry-go-round for 16 years. After numerous rehabs, countless CAC and therapy sessions, and innumerable 12-step meetings, he could not shake the bonds of his addiction, and no one would, or could, teach him how to do it. Actually, there was nothing to teach. Indoctrinated in The Truth, Wayne was to work The Program and "expect miracles"—expect God to save him. An AA slogan puts this succinctly: "I can't, He can, I think I'll let Him." The Big Book is wordier, but the underlying concept is the same:.

> He stood in the Presence of Infinite Power and Love . . . For the first time, he lived in conscious companionship with his Creator. . . . His alcoholic problem was taken away. . . . God had restored his sanity.

Wayne's World

Wayne lived in the merry-go-round world of recovery for many years. Deeply indoctrinated with The Truth, it was difficult for him to imagine life any other way. But bit by bit he began fighting for his freedom, and his life. After years of disillusionment, Wayne is now discovering the other side of The Truth:

> I have seen and experienced it all. I doubt there is much I can add to what you already know about the mindlessness I have experienced in AA and rehabs at the hands of sickos and bullies. I am tired of being beat up. In my first rehab, they tried to dumb me down. They said my vocabulary was too good. Imagine that. When I asked what this has to do with recovery, I was attacked with sarcasm and accusations of "having all the answers." In another center, I was called before the community for reading a book by Albert Ellis, non-approved literature. I had to surrender the book or be discharged. I did say the book

was about getting well from addictive behavior, but it was as if I'd brought in a book about building bombs and blowing up bridges. That probably would have been met with less resistance.

I spent an hour debating with my landlady about why AA has not worked for me. She is an AA member. I got nowhere. Of course, there is nothing wrong with AA and something is wrong with me. I must avoid these types of conversations with the AA Moonies. She accused me of being closed-minded ignoring the fact that I was open-minded to AA for sixteen years. I suggested it was she who was being closed-minded for insisting AA was the only way. Not surprisingly, I still got nowhere.

Wayne's well-being doesn't concern merry-go-round operators. Should he suffer for another 16 years, if he lives that long, at least he'd be "in recovery" and working The Program just as The Truth says he should—even though he'd continue to be miserable and to relapse.

Psychologist Albert Ellis's blacklisted book violated the center's strict information control decree. New information, no matter how beneficial, even lifesaving, must be suppressed swiftly and decisively. Confiscate it, sequester it, destroy it, and it no longer exists. The Truth is upheld.

Wayne was right. Books on bomb building or blowing up bridges would be met with less resistance. Building bombs and blowing up bridges doesn't threaten The Truth.

The Truth Keepers—Defenders of The Truth

Truth keepers come from all walks of life and are relentless when promoting and defending Bill Wilson's Truth. Some are innocent operators who naively sanction The Truth when they steer addicted family and friends into AA and "treatment." But most are AA members and/or professional operators who earn their livings in the addiction treatment field.

Truth keepers wear many hats: TV and movie celebrities, addiction therapists, alcohol and drug counselors, authors, clergy, clerks, judges, newspaper columnists, police officers, politicians, radio personalities, program sponsors, sports stars, taxi drivers, your best in-Program "pals," your neighbors. Truth keepers are especially vocal outside the familiar turf of their rehab centers and 12-step meeting rooms. And as you learned from Wayne, truth keepers can even masquerade as landladies.

Truth-Keeping Tactics

The RGM slogan, "There are none too dumb for the AA program, but many are too smart," is unintentionally revealing. Independent thinking is verboten and is met with attacks. "If you're so bright, why are you here instead of sober out there?" embodies the futility of attempting to discuss The Truth with the truth keepers. Ridiculing intelligence, "dumbing down," and intimidation are the truth keepers' stock in trade. Judge for yourself whether or not this is "humble" behavior.

Those subjected to the "humble" behavior of RGM operators go through a humiliating ordeal. It's a perverse attempt at ego deflation, for the sole purpose of getting its victims to accept The Truth. In fact, healthy egos are abhorrent to the truth keepers because, in their own words, "EGO = Ease God Out"—yet another of their catchy slogans.

Information control, and to a lesser degree physical control, must continue after clients leave rehab. Outpatient aftercare programs address this concern. These programs reaffirm your powerlessness and need for divine guidance, while extolling the redeeming quality of The Truth.

One form of aftercare is halfway houses. Here, (often coerced) clients knuckle down to life according to Bill, and get their own personal truth keeper: a sponsor. Also, all inductees must attend three months of daily AA meetings: 90 meetings in 90 days. This extended control is believed essential for the brainwashing—sorry, I mean, for The Truth—to sink in. Miss one meeting and The Truth will pass you by. You'd need to start the "90 in 90" over or risk a lifetime of misery. You'll see why soon.

The Morgue

The standard AA prediction is "jails, institutions, or death" for those who don't accept The Truth. Through mock funerals, truth-keeping addiction counselors attempt to bully clients to accept their morbid prediction as true. Performed in rehab center seclusion, an inductee who shows signs of independence is singled out to "lie in state." Searching for a few sincere words, the "mourning" rehab community files by their "deceased" comrade. This is treatment?

Booze, other drugs, or destructive addictive behavior had nothing to do with "killing" their friend. It was his or her failure to accept The Truth.

The Truth Must Be True

"Take what you can use and leave the rest," is one of AA's most hypocritical slogans. Everything from parking tickets to relapse is traced to "not working a good program," or not following some "suggestion" you should have used, but didn't. Your sin of omission is the truth keeper's lever. Not doing "90 in 90" is a case in point. A relapse, for example, is traced to your not completing that daily regimen. But what happens when you complete the "90 in 90" and still relapse? Truth keepers simply shift the focus to some other aspect of The Program you should have used, but didn't, or some other "suggestion" you didn't take. Perhaps you failed to perform your fourth-step "fearless moral inventory" fearlessly enough, or you "left something out" of your fifth-step confession. In other words, The Program is perfect. It has all the answers. It always works if properly worked. If you relapse or have other problems, the fault is *always* yours, never The Program's.

How do truth keepers indoctrinate newcomers with The Truth outside of rehab centers? Your neighborhood 12-step meetings take care of that. Every community houses truth keepers. To keep you coming back, they exploit your vulnerability by dangling The Truth, with its threats and promises, like a carrot on a stick. "Bring your body and your mind will follow," is a common ploy. Once they have you in "the rooms," their anti-independent-thinking crusade begins: "Take the cotton out of your ears and stick it in your mouth," "Your best thinking got you here," "Utilize, don't analyze," they chant. But with heightened perception, liberated merry-go-round riders like Wayne can decipher the chant: "Shut-up while we force-feed you our Truth and nothing but our Truth."

For truth keepers, the Big Book is their bible and The Program is their religion. Both are unassailable. Like other true believers, they will do almost anything to maintain proper respect for their sacred beliefs—including forcing them down the throats of coerced, recalcitrant newcomers.

By refusing to develop heightened perception, truth keepers elect to close their eyes, ears and minds to anything other than their own beliefs. They do this in the name of God, sobriety, and "rigorous honesty." This validates their very existence. Your existence is of little consequence. If you need a reminder of that, think back to those trained in The Truth, but who are no longer with us. From Chapter 1 of this book:

> While it's too late [for] Chris, Jerry, Curt, Andy, Hugh, Brynn, Darrell, Phil, and Terri, it's not too late for you. So run, run away as far as possible and fast as you can from anyone who tells you that Alcoholics Anonymous and its 12-step program is the only road to recovery or the best way to recover.

The Other Side of The Truth

The next chapter analyzes the RGM buzzwords denial, dependence, blackout, tolerance, preoccupation, intervention, and loss of control. All are defined and explained. We'll also consider a phenomenon overlooked by the addiction experts, "anticipation." You will learn its meaning and how it affects your addictive behavior. You'll see the differences between healthy and unhealthy addictions and between psychological dependence and chemical dependence. You'll gain new insights into alcoholism and addiction and discover that there's a logical sequence (one you can break) which leads to addiction, and that it's not a progression of an incurable disease.

Chapter 6

Sticks & Stones:
Words That Can Hurt

"We cannot solve problems with the same thinking we had
when we created the problems"
—Albert Einstein

The decision to quit alcohol or other drugs is intensely personal. While you know you should stop, deep inside you have a foreboding, a sense of loss. Why do the good times associated with drinking outshine the devastation of the bad? Why do we dream of successfully drinking, as everyone else does? Isn't it curious that the mere thought of quitting can evoke anxiety, even as we recall the pain and misfortune caused by our past drinking? Thoughts of this nature mean one thing only: dependence. If you didn't depend on using some chemical, quitting wouldn't matter much to you. Really.

Brussel Sprouts

Think of it this way, and keep your heightened perception tuned up: How would you react if brussel sprouts were cut from your diet? While you may like them, would purging them from your life cause great anxiety? The answer is "yes" if you've come to depend on brussel sprouts. But the odds that you depend on brussel sprouts are slim to none. Why? Because you have no particular attachment to brussel sprouts. They weren't a staple at birthdays, weddings, and other special occasions. Advertising hasn't inundated you with promises about the rewards of eating brussel sprouts. You never raised a glass of brussel sprouts on New Year's Eve. Brussel sprouts were not included in your religious services. They weren't glamorized in movies and on television. They were never there to greet you after a trying day. They didn't ease tension and alter your consciousness.

Society never touted brussel sprouts as sexy, sophisticated, or a necessary adjunct to your enjoyment of life. They have never fulfilled a need in your life, real or imagined. You simply are not dependent on brussel sprouts. Ah, but alcohol! It has played a major role in your life. It was your faithful companion during good times and bad. You came to depend on it, and your own extensive use and society's alluring portrayals strongly reinforced that dependence

Dependence: Healthy vs. Unhealthy

Dependence is a double-edged sword. Depending on chemicals to control blood pressure, cholesterol, or blood sugar can improve the quality of life. But a dependence on self-prescribed, "feel good" chemicals often does the opposite, and the dependency can lead to addiction.

Anyone can become dependent on just about anything. One condition need only be prolonged use. For example, you depend on your car to start every day. You depend on the utility company to supply your home with electricity. You depend on barbers to cut your hair. You depend on a grocer to supply your food. Or do you?

Let's try a different perspective, a heightened perception: We expect our cars to start and depend on them for transportation. We expect utility companies to provide electricity and depend on that electricity to power equipment. We expect grocers to provide food and depend on that for our dietary needs. We expect barbers to cut hair and depend on their skill.

By extension, we expect alcohol and other drugs to provide a service (feeling good/alleviating misery, serving as a social lubricant) and depend on that service. People abusing booze/chemicals have trouble perceiving that the service alcohol once provided (easing tension, facilitating socializing) has developed into a disservice. The once faithful companion has become the faithless enemy. Psychologically dependent people aren't fully conscious of this yet, but they're not in denial either. Their heightened perception is in very poor repair. So, they continue abusing alcohol or other drugs, expecting the "good service" they provided in the good old days.

Cars, utility companies, barbers, and grocers play a significant role in your life. You depend on what they provide. Unlike alcohol, they are not destructive. They improve the quality of your life, as do medicines that control blood sugar or cholesterol.

Dependence then, is a state of psychological or physical dependence, or both. Unlike brussel sprouts (food), automobiles (possessions/transportation), or grocers (people), alcohol is a psychoactive drug that changes your consciousness.

If you're reading this book because of your alcohol use, over time you developed a reliance on that chemically fueled change of consciousness. You might have become so dependent that you lost your freedom to function unless fortified with alcohol or other drugs. ("I need it just to feel normal.") You might have reached the point where you drank not only during stressful times, but also to feel a semblance of calm or happiness. You become psychologically dependent, physically dependent, or both.

Tolerance, The Hollow Leg

Developing tolerance to alcohol is a hallmark of physical dependence. Tolerance occurs when the amount of alcohol usually ingested no longer produces the desired effect. The liver breaks down alcohol at a faster rate than prior to the development of physical dependence, necessitating a greater intake to achieve the same level in the blood (BAL—blood-alcohol level). At the same time, nerve cells in the brain become less responsive to a given amount of alcohol. (If you've been drinking heavily, had this occur, and since then have a reduced tolerance, getting blasted on very little alcohol, you have reason to worry—this reversal came about as the result of physical damage. The good news here, if you've reached this stage, is that you are not powerless, diseased, or hopelessly addicted. You can always decide to stop drinking; and you can stay stopped. Many others who have reached this stage have done exactly that.)

Mild tolerance also develops in the social drinker, but it is commonly seen in its more extreme form in the heavy drinker who can "hold his liquor." The alcohol dependent, however, are often not only tolerant, but in many cases need increased doses just to feel normal.

More Disease Hype

There is much debate over the disease concept of alcoholism/addiction. While the RGM calls alcoholism and other chemical addictions incurable progressive diseases, a great many others do not. Rutgers University philosophy professor and author, Bruce W.

Wilshire, examines this issue in his book, *Wild Hunger: The Primal Roots of Modern Addiction:*

[A] great price is paid for treating addictions as a disease. Conscience is the sense of right and wrong and the feeling of responsibility. It is softened, but also the overall sense of self is reduced—the immediate sense of oneself as an ongoing source of initiatives in the world, a real power, an agent. Reduced or lost is meaningful ecstatic involvements, and the sense of responsibility that goes with them.

To regard addiction as a disease is well intentioned, but it is a de facto insult to human beings. It is symptomatic of the corporate, addicted consumer society which fails to acknowledge the total capacities of human beings—individuals who need responsibility, self-direction, and meaning in life.

The simple fact that "treatment" for this supposedly chronic, incurable "disease" hinges on submission to AA and the religious musings of Bill Wilson sends up red flags. Actually, it sends up flares, rockets, and missiles. Some say it borders on voodoo.

Incredibly, given that the "disease" definition of addiction rests on nothing but assertion, the National Institute on Drug Abuse, National Institutes of Health, classifies addiction as a "chronic relapsing brain disease." As innocent operators will do, award-winning journalist Bill Moyers echoed this view in his 1998 PBS special, "Addiction: Close to Home." Moyers' son, William Cope, a self-labeled "grateful, recovering alcoholic and addict," had been through the mill of multiple rehab stays and 12-step indoctrinations, and finally converted to the AA religion; he is now a "card carrying" Bill Wilson groupie. And his dad loyally echoes the party line. Moyers, and those like him who advance the disease concept, have not provided one iota of evidence that addiction is a "disease," let alone a "chronic relapsing brain disease." All that they've done is assert that it is—over, and over, and over. The fact that a good majority of the American public accept the idea that alcoholism/addiction is a disease proves one thing, and one thing only: that Hitler's "big lie" technique can work—repeat a lie continually, squelch dissenting voices, and most people will eventually come to believe the lie.

What Is This Thing Called Alcoholism?

Alcoholism is behavior, complete with concepts, rituals, and philosophies. The RGM acknowledges these behavioral aspects of their mythical disease. The "recovering" often say, "I've beaten the 'alcohol' part of this thing, now I have to deal with the 'ism' part." Former first lady, and self-labeled "recovering alcoholic," Betty Ford, has advanced this position for years. In a 1992 interview conducted at her Betty Ford Center in Rancho Mirage, California, she stated: "When I was a practicing alcoholic, my family especially the children were very able to manipulate me."

"Practicing alcoholic" suggests a contrived lifestyle adopted by people dependent on alcohol. It suggests behavior, not disease. Think about it. The intention of Bill Wilson's 12-step program, as Betty Ford promotes it, is to change your beliefs. Through the study and application of Bill's doctrine, practicing and living the alcoholic lifestyle is supposed to be replaced by the supposedly healthier "AA way of life." That doesn't happen for most. So, what's a "recovering alcoholic" to do if this "miracle" doesn't happen? Hop on the recovery merry-go-round and strap yourself in, because it's back to the Betty Ford Center for you.

A Matter of Definitions

The *Merck Manual of Medical Information,* (Sept. 1999) defines alcoholism as follows:

> A chronic disease characterized by a tendency to drink more than was intended, unsuccessful attempts at stopping drinking and continued drinking despite adverse social and occupational consequences.

No empirical evidence supports this definition. While the characteristics are accurate, "chronic disease" is not. Replace "chronic disease" with "behavior" or "lifestyle" and the definition radically changes.
Look:

Alcoholism: A behavior/lifestyle characterized by a tendency to drink more than was intended, unsuccessful attempts at stopping drinking and continued drinking despite adverse social and occupational consequences.

Membership in Bill Wilson's religious sobriety society is not required for making changes in your behavior or lifestyle. For that matter, recovery from chronic disease doesn't require it either. The RGM's spiritual remedy does not address how to quit drinking or end any addiction. Nowhere in the 12-steps is it even suggested that you quit drinking, or even try. In fact, you're taught to quit trying, to instead surrender, and to "expect a miracle." This is the program of a religious-conversion organization, not an addiction-ending organization. Remember, their goal is to convert you, not cure you.

The disease of alcoholism is the $10-billion-a-year addiction treatment industry's cash cow. It means billions in insurance dollars, tax breaks, government programs, and grants.

But tap into your heightened perception and think of it this way— even if alcoholism were the chronic disease posited by Merck, and you exhibit the characteristics as described, wouldn't it be in your best interest to learn how to overcome it? And if it were not the chronic disease they propose, and you exhibit the characteristics as described, wouldn't it still be in your best interest to learn how to overcome it? Whether or not alcoholism/addiction is a disease or not, the long-standing problem is that recovery merry-go-round operators will never teach you to overcome it; they will only teach you to endure it while "recovering" and praying for a "miracle."

From Use to Addiction to Recovery Mania

The *Merck Manual* defines addiction as follows:

The compulsive activity and overwhelming involvement with a specific activity. The activity may be gambling or may involve the use of almost any substance, such as a drug. Drugs can cause either psychologic dependence or both psychologic and physical dependence.

This definition is good, but doesn't go far enough. A better, amended definition would read:

Addiction: The compulsive activity and overwhelming involvement with a specific activity. The activity may be gambling or may involve the use of almost any substance, such as a drug. Drugs can cause either a psychologic dependence or both psychologic and physical dependence. Addicts continue their addictive activity, often escalating it, despite knowing the severe personal and/or social problems it causes them.[1]

There is a logical sequence leading to addiction; it is not a "disease" progression: use leads to tolerance, tolerance leads to abuse, and abuse leads to dependence and addiction.

A very wide range of compulsive behaviors fit this sequence, and AA's spin-off groups address a wide range of these. Gamblers Anonymous (GA) and Overeaters Anonymous (OA) are two examples. These groups modify the steps to suit their purpose. They replace "alcohol" (in AA's original 12-steps) with their concern. For instance, see GA's step 1: "We admitted we were powerless over gambling, that our lives had become unmanageable"; and OA's step 1: "We admitted we were powerless over food, that our lives had become unmanageable." But the RGM doesn't stop with gaming or groceries. There are 12-step programs for almost every human problem imaginable:

Addicted Jews in Recovery Anonymous
Addictions Anonymous
Adrenaline Addicts Anonymous
Benzodiazapines Anonymous
Caffeine Anonymous
Clutterers Anonymous
Compulsive Eaters Anonymous
Debtors Anonymous
Depressives Anonymous
Diabetics Anonymous
Dual Disorders Anonymous
Eating Addictions Anonymous
Fear of Success Anonymous

---

1. Addictions can be positive or negative, despite their compulsive nature. Positive addictions to exercising, eating only healthy foods, or to learning a new language, for example, can improve the quality of life. For the purpose of this book, addictions are viewed as negative, therefore the amended definition.

Food Addicts Anonymous
Food Addicts in Recovery Anonymous
Helping Cross Dressers Anonymous
Humans Anonymous
Impotents Anonymous
Incest Survivors Anonymous
International Nurses Anonymous
International Pharmacists Anonymous
Junk Food Anonymous
Kleptomaniacs Anonymous
Marijuana Anonymous
Messies Anonymous
Methadone Anonymous
Nicotine Anonymous
Prostitutes Anonymous
Racism and Bigotry Anonymous
Self-Mutilators Anonymous
Sex and Love Addicts Anonymous
Sex Workers Anonymous
Sexaholics Anonymous
Sexual Compulsives Anonymous
Sexual Recovery Anonymous
Shoplifters Anonymous
Sinners Anonymous
Spenders Anonymous
Sucrose Addicts Anonymous
Suicide Anonymous
Transsexuals Anonymous
Vulgarity Anonymous
Workaholics Anonymous

The very diversity of this list is strong evidence that AA's 12-step "program" is a religious-conversion program, not an addiction-recovery program. (Can you imagine anyone being "addicted" to being impotent, an incest survivor, or a transsexual?)

As stated in Chapter 1, "If you can abuse it, somebody will want to term it a disease and put you in a program to overcome it." Admitting powerlessness over your racism, kleptomania, shoplifting, impotence, spending, self-mutilating, sexual compulsions, even your own suicidal thoughts, is not in your best interest. It keeps you vulnerable and dependent on equally vulnerable and dependent groupers. It can also have grave consequences, for you or another, when your "powerlessness" leads you to "act out" your "uncontrollable" urges. But none of these behaviors are "diseases," and you don't need lifelong "recovery" to overcome them.

If I'm Denyin', I'm Lyin'

How important are drugs/alcohol in your life? Think about your own experiences. Are they an integral part of your social life? Your solitary activities? Could you take a vacation and enjoy yourself without using drugs or alcohol? Picture yourself relaxing and enjoying your leisure time. Is there a drink in your hand? Picture yourself at a sporting event, wedding reception or concert. Is there a drink or drug in your hand? Picture yourself on "the day after." Is there a drink in your hand?

If the change of consciousness alcohol provides has become essential to your lifestyle, you'll expect to drink at receptions, ballgames, parties, and after a funeral or a hard day. But you don't expect to drink on the cotton-mouthed, head splitting "day after," yet there's a drink in your hand. Anyone can become chemically dependent if he or she drinks or uses a drug long enough and at high enough doses. Yet addressing this dependence is often back-burnered even in the wake of failed relationships, failing health, family turmoil, financial woes, job loss, social fiascos, and trouble with the law, including car wrecks and DUIs.

Failure to associate these negative experiences with alcohol/drug abuse is termed "denial" by the recovery group movement. It's a refusal to accept your dependence/addiction because you don't "see" it. This "denial" is apparent when you're asked to divulge the particulars of your alcohol/drug use—frequency of use, amount or quantities used, where, with whom, even why. Honest answers are rarely forthcoming. How many times have you heard, "I can handle it, I don't have a problem, and I can quit any time I want?" Perhaps you've said it yourself.

Understand this: Alcoholics and addicts are not "in denial" as defined by the RGM. Rather, they lie; and they lie a lot. While lying isn't as clinical sounding as "denial," it is what alcoholics/addicts do, and there is no deep, mysterious reason behind it begging for "treatment." A part of alcoholics/addicts knows that they are hooked and can't imagine life without their stuff. Part of them loathes this and desperately wants to quit, but they are ambivalent over their alcohol/drug abuse. Ambivalence is not denial. The addicted part never wants the party to end, hence, the lying. I address this ambivalence and show how to identify and overcome the addicted part in chapters 9 and 10.

Intervention

The whole twisted concept of denial paves they way for harmful, ill-conceived, and badly executed "interventions." An intervention is thought to be a loving, well intentioned way of telling your "out of control" alcoholic, in a group setting, the extent to which the drinking is affecting his or her life, as well as your own. Concerned family and friends rehearse their speeches, outlining specific consequences should the alcoholic/addict refuse treatment. Divorce, no contact with children, and shunning by friends are examples. Job loss is also often threatened when bosses and co-workers are involved.

Interventions do not arise spontaneously. RGM "professionals" are almost always involved, and are ready to whisk the victim away to 12-step treatment at the end of the intervention. The goal is always the same: bushwhack the boozer, browbeat him or her into submission, and trundle the boozer into treatment. Family and friends don't realize (until it's too late, if they ever do) that "treatment" consists of coercive religious indoctrination. And it's the "Treatment Works" campaigns which deceive them into steering their addicted loved ones into the clutches of recovery merry-go-round operators disguised as selfless interventionists.

Interventions often backfire. While family intent is genuinely benign, the degrading confrontation leaves their addicted loved one with a dubious choice: treatment or else! And if he or she has had treatment, he or she knows what's coming: AA and the recovery merry-go-round. Unless the addicted loved one is immediately shipped off to rehab after an intervention, he or she may take "powerlessness" to its extreme. He or she may drink or drug into oblivion, never learning that there are healthy alternatives to drinking/drugging and to year after year of dreary 12-step meetings and the constant fear of relapsing.

Parts of the Process

Researchers study the physical, social, and psychological correlates of the alcohol addiction process. They've studied everything from vitamin deficiencies, to genetics, to family structure, to retirement blues. Yet, three common elements, and one overlooked element, all need clarification:

1) **Loss of control** does not mean powerlessness. Loss of control does not mean that taking a drink will automatically result in a binge. Loss of control does not mean that the alcoholic will always get drunk once drinking begins. (The RGM advances a different position: "It's the first drink that gets you drunk," put more colloquially, "One drink, one drunk." This very dangerous and irresponsible prediction often becomes a self-fulfilling prophecy, especially for the naive newcomer who is already battling to curb his or her desires.) Loss of control does mean that the alcoholic cannot accurately predict when he or she will or will not drink to intoxication once drinking starts. For many, this fact alone is a great quit-for-good motivator once they perceive the reality of this phenomenon, usually through trial and error, or inconsistent results with controlled drinking.

2) **Blackouts** are an alcohol-induced amnesia, synonymous with memory loss. They are not the same as "passing out." Blackouts are common and somewhat accepted by society. Some people will laugh over the fact that the night before they did "something silly," but can't remember it. Others will not laugh when confronted with their alcohol-induced misdeeds. Former "Tonight Show" bandleader Doc Severinsen speaks of the numerous occasions he drove from New York City to his home in Larchmont, about 40 miles away. He'd wake up at home, but could not remember getting his car, leaving the parking garage, driving through midtown streets, driving on the highway, or paying tolls. Because of their frequency and nature, blackouts alone don't signify chemical dependence or addiction. However, their increased frequency in a particular individual could indicate an impending dependence and/or addiction.

3) **Preoccupation** is absorption with obtaining alcohol/drugs. The hunt for supply is paramount in the addicted lifestyle, and addicts will often do virtually anything to obtain their substance of choice. To avoid the pangs and possibly dangerous complications of withdrawal, preserving a supply can mean as little as having the next fix or a hidden bottle. While acquiring alcohol/drugs becomes a high in itself, the anticipation of the real high to come is the driving force behind preoccupation.

4) Anticipation—the part they forgot. Overlooked by the addiction experts, anticipation is a subset of preoccupation. It's not the same as an urge or a craving. Let's examine this. Preoccupation means that you'll want liquor available at your cousin's wedding. If it's not to be served, you may: a) not attend; b) bring your own; c) attend under duress and have a miserable time.

Anticipation occurs when you know booze will be served. So, you'll anxiously sit through the wedding ceremony in gleeful anticipation of the fun you'll have once drinking begins, and you feel the effects. There's no "hunt" involved, and it's not the same as thinking about the food, dancing or festivities. Anticipation foresees the chemical effects of a psychoactive drug, simply put, your anticipation of a guaranteed drunk or high.

We see this phenomenon when people, "can't wait" for quitting time, the kids to go to bed, the mid-day bridge game, the weekend, Monday night football, classes to end, the barbecue, the picnic, the party. Again, there is no "hunt." A supply is assured, so the focus shifts to anticipating the chemical's effects. While responsible drinking is acceptable in many settings, ask yourself if the anticipation of getting drunk/high is your motivation for even attending these functions in the first place. In other words, would you still hang out at the bar five nights a week just for the company? Additionally, ask yourself if the anticipation of getting loaded is your focus until the time you actually partake.

This little story sums of the phenomenon of anticipation: I remember a fellow who loved to go deep-sea fishing. He rarely spoke of his sport the way one might expect of an enthusiast, but when a trip was coming up, it was all he talked about. Some years later, an old friend asked him about his great love, deep-sea fishing. It seems the one-time angler never really cared that much for fishing and hadn't gone in years. "Since I quit drinking I realized it wasn't the fishing I loved. It was the deep-sea drinking."

Anticipation and expectation are not the same. Expectation implies a strong belief that an event will occur: "The lights will go on when I hit the switch." Anticipation, as part of the addiction process, eagerly awaits the feeling. But the event—reception, ballgame, barbeque, dance, party—is really an excuse for the feeling: intoxication. It's clear that anticipation is fundamental to chemical dependence and addiction.

You now know what you're up against. Whether you are abusing, dependent on, or addicted to alcohol/drugs, you will learn to change the thinking and behavior that got you there—without treatment or "recovery." But first, you need to make an important decision, and the next chapter asks you to do that. It gives special attention to those of you still physically dependent/addicted, special attention that's intended to help you make your decision. If you're ready, then it's time to turn the page. If important decisions aren't in the cards for you today, then sleep on it tonight. Be it today or tomorrow, the decision only you can make will be waiting.

Chapter 7

Decision Day: When Quitting Means Winning

"The virtue of all achievement is victory over oneself. Those who
know this can never know defeat."
—A.J. Cronin

No one drinks in joyful anticipation of the morning after. While a
couple of aspirin and 24 hours is the remedy for most, it's not as
straightforward for the alcohol dependent. For them, the desire to
intoxicate, often to avoid the discomfort of withdrawal, can super-
sede the most basic human needs. Friendship, family, food, career,
sex, even personal hygiene can all take a back seat to the bottle.

But you've decided to quit, for good. What now? If you're physically dependent, by enduring a few days of misery (withdrawal),
you'll be avoiding a lifetime of addiction hell. For the majority of
people who do stop, serious complications seldom occur. Even so, if
you're physically dependent on alcohol you should consult a doctor
before detoxing.

Alcohol Detox & Withdrawal

Withdrawal is no fun. It's not pleasant. It can be difficult, but it's
not *too* difficult. It is a manageable process, and many people weath-
er the storm by going "cold turkey." However, medically supervised
detox is available and effective. With medications to aid the detox
process, even the most severe cases are successfully treated.
Although there is no one perfect medication, a class of drugs called
benzodiazapines, (Librium, Valium) are often used, both because
they are emotionally calming and because they have anticonvulsant
properties. Doses are gradually reduced as withdrawal symptoms
subside. Vitamins are administered and based on patient need, espe-

cially potassium, magnesium, and the B-vitamin thiamine. There can be complications if the person being detoxed used other drugs, prescription or non-prescription, in addition to alcohol. No one knows the extent of your alcohol abuse better than you do. If you have any doubt as to your well-being when you stop, seek medical advice.[1]

The usual withdrawal period from alcohol is three to seven days. Physically, you are not addicted to alcohol after that time. Studies show that some people suffer sleep disturbances weeks after detoxing, but the causes have not been determined, nor do all who end their drinking experience these disturbances. Suffice it to say that you might not sleep like a baby right after quitting, but then again you might.

The bottom line is that you're going to feel lousy for a few days, but the discomfort is negligible compared to a lifetime (possibly a short one) of addiction. Here's a tip: Forcefully reminding yourself that withdrawal symptoms are temporary will help. Think of it as your body doling out some serious payback for all the junk you've been feeding it. Know, as surely as the sun rises, that whatever you're feeling, physically and emotionally, is a transition phase to wellness.

Major & Minor Withdrawal

The two categories of withdrawal are minor and major, minor meaning early withdrawal and major meaning late. The severity of minor withdrawal varies greatly based on the amount and duration of alcohol used. The body eliminates alcohol at approximately one ounce per hour. Due to this rapid elimination, you could experience any, or just possibly all, of the following: agitation; blurred vision; early morning waking; headache; high blood pressure; insomnia; mild tremors; nausea; numbness of the extremities; sweating; vivid dreaming; and vomiting. Exacerbated by little or no sleep, anxiety can be acute. A general sense of foreboding is common, as alcohol is a CNS (central nervous system) depressant. Symptoms can begin

---

1. Some rehabilitation centers include treatment after detox. If you choose that route, be aware of the intense 12-step/AA indoctrination you will be "treated" with. If you have been on the rehab merry-go-round, I'm sure this comes as no surprise to you. But rehabs are not your only option. A variety of medical facilities, including hospitals and clinics, perform detox. If you need to detox, I'd advise calling your doctor or local hospital and telling them that you desire detox services, not addiction treatment.

within a few hours after stopping alcohol, are usually gone after 48, and typically peak from 24 to 36 hours after the last drink.

The above symptoms are typical of minor withdrawal and generally do not require medical intervention.

Alleviating Minor Withdrawal Symptoms

Because of the changes and adaptations your body has made to accommodate the bombardment of alcohol, it's helpful to know what to expect, and what you can do to help yourself during minor withdrawal. Time is your prescription and the use of over-the-counter analgesics or stomach remedies can alleviate much of your discomfort. More severe cases often require drinking extra fluids. When quenching your thirst, stay away from caffeinated drinks and citrus juices such as orange and grapefruit. Caffeine can make you edgy, and the acids in citrus juices can irritate your stomach. Cranberry juice and sports drinks are good as is, of course, water. Use carbonated beverages such as ginger ale at your discretion. Eat small, light meals when you can. Soup and crackers seem tolerable during minor withdrawal, so be sure to have them available. If you smoke, try keeping it to a minimum. Your body/liver has enough cleansing work to do without more toxins from cigarettes. (You can address your smoking habit after you've gone through withdrawal.) Rest as much as possible.

Seizures, though infrequent, occur during minor withdrawal. They are an indicator that major withdrawal will most likely follow. However, it is not necessary to have a seizure for major withdrawal to develop. Again, if you are in any doubt as to your well-being, seek proper medical attention, especially if you are over 45 years old and if you suffer from complications due to other illnesses.

Major Withdrawal

Major (late) withdrawal is synonymous with Delirium Tremens (DTs). It develops gradually as the symptoms of early withdrawal dissipate, but can appear in as little as 24 hours. Major withdrawal peaks 72 to 96 hours after the last drink. DTs are potentially life threatening. Medically supervised detox is your best and safest bet. Even with seizure as an indicator, you can't be sure if major withdrawal will develop or not. Predicting DTs is not an exact science.

Here, the old adage, "better safe than sorry," is more than apropos. Seek medical advice regarding your condition. While you can quit booze and stay quit without addiction treatment or recovery, a comprehensive detox and withdrawal plan makes sense, and is recommended for anyone with any level of physical dependence.

DTs are rare. They develop in fewer then 5% of hospital patients in early alcohol withdrawal. Clinical features of DTs include disorientation; confusion; psychomotor over activity (muscle movement resulting from mental processes, i.e. spasms, twitching); autonomic over activity (non-voluntary functions of the nervous system originating in the spinal column affecting heart, glands, stomach, intestines); distorted sensory perception (where you "see" things that aren't there); and auditory hallucinations (where you "hear" things that aren't there).

In addition to the classic little green men and pink elephants, everything from bats to bugs, from bears to slugs, have been "seen." Walls may move. Wallpaper patterns may begin to ebb and flow. Music, sirens, horns, beeping sounds, humming and voices have all been reported as being "heard." It can be a very trying period, both physically and emotionally. With proper medical diagnosis and care, fatal reactions to DTs are extremely rare today. Again, age and co-existing medical conditions can complicate recovery from Delirium Tremens.

Drug Withdrawal

Never take drug withdrawal lightly. Prescription drug withdrawal is usually a step-down process that doctors will help you with. And you absolutely must seek medical aid to withdraw from some drugs, such as methadone, where withdrawal can kill you. As with booze, drug withdrawal can be difficult, but always remember that withdrawal is temporary, and your freedom from drugs will be permanent. There is, however, much debate in the addiction field regarding street drugs. Some researchers believe that the more severe the physical withdrawal, the more dangerous the drug must be. Crack cocaine and methamphetamine are examples of two highly abused drugs, yet the physical symptoms accompanying their withdrawal are minimal. Even heroin withdrawal is managed with appropriate medication, although many addicts successfully tough it out going cold turkey. Once more, check with your doctor if there's any doubt as to your well-being before you stop. Make Decision Day one of many great days to come.

Decision Time

Have you heard the one about the salesman, the housewife, the politician, and the hobo? No this isn't some old joke; all four were addicted to booze.

The once-stellar salesman had disintegrated into a red-eyed, disheveled shell of a man. His articulate sales pitch had crumbled into an inarticulate claptrap of disjointed phrases. Thoughts of "one more sale, just one more big score" drove him. That's all he wanted. Then he'd be able to face his addiction; then he'd be ready to quit.

The homemaker had alienated herself from family and friends. Her drinking had pushed nearly everyone away. Even her husband and children kept their distance because mom had become so unpredictable. She knew that her affair with booze was the root of her troubles. She also knew that quitting was her best hope for salvaging her tenuous relationships. But at the same time, she felt her relationships needed mending first. That's all she wanted. Then she'd be able to face her addiction; then she'd be ready to quit.

The politician seemed to live a charmed life. Successful in the eyes of the public, he was quick with a handshake and a smile. Eventually, the smiles turned into frowns and the handshakes into jitters. His skills eroded, prompting rash judgments. His private life became public due to questionable behavior and associations. Like the others, he knew his troubles stemmed from the bottle. Still, he wanted his popularity back. "A rise in the polls," that's all he wanted. Then he'd be able to face his addiction; then he'd be ready to quit.

The down-on-his-luck hobo was awash in cheap wine. Hand to mouth and shelter to shelter, his existence was a blurred succession of handouts and cons. Any opportunity for betterment was wasted as his brown-bagged elixir never left his side. "Can't I get a break?" he'd lament. "Just one break," that's all he wanted. Then he'd be able to face his addiction; then he'd be ready to quit.

No Time Like The Present

So, is it decision day yet? Are you ready to face your addiction now and stop the procrastination? The salesman, the homemaker, the politician, and the hobo all had the same attitude when it came to quitting. All wanted something before they would quit. What they failed to perceive was that waiting for the "right" condition before quitting means that that day may never come. And should their conditions be met, they would likely "forget" about quitting, thinking that they made too big a deal out of the whole situation in the first place. So, again I ask you: Is it decision day yet? Are you ready to tough it out for a few days to gain a lifetime of freedom from booze? Remember, the majority of those who quit drinking do not suffer the extremes of withdrawal. Still, should that be the case, know that it is temporary, that you're not alone, and that it will pass. The rewards are well worth it.

Once you stop, though, you'll need to understand and overcome the pleasure-seeking attitudes and behaviors that linger after withdrawal is complete. This doesn't require a lifetime of recovery meetings, as you'll see in the next chapter.

Chapter 8

Discovery: Building Your Foundation

"Learn as if you were to live forever."
—Ghandi

Now that you've stopped, you want to stay stopped. Traditionally this has meant constant reminders of your supposed powerlessness over alcohol by other like-minded "recovering" folk in the perpetual cycle of AA meetings. There, you could contemplate the mystery of your disease while swilling bad coffee and recalling the horrors of your drinking past. You could also "help" others by urging them to turn their lives and wills over to the Higher Powers of the Wilson religion. Let's go back to the Big Book:

> [T]he main problem of the alcoholic centers in his mind, rather than his body. If you ask him why he started on that last bender, the chances are he will offer you any one of a hundred alibis . . . Once in a while he may tell the truth. And the truth, strange to say, is usually that he has no more idea why he took that first drink than you have. Some drinkers have excuses with which they are satisfied part of the time. But in their hearts they really do not know why they do it. Once this malady has a real hold, they are a baffled lot.

Later the Big Book relates the story of Jim:

> He had much knowledge about himself as an alcoholic. Yet all reasons for not drinking were easily pushed aside in favor of the foolish idea that he could take whiskey if only he mixed it with milk!

Both excerpts promote the idea that the alcoholic is utterly powerlessness over booze, is utterly powerless to prevent himself from indulging in another drinking debacle. No wonder they "[we]re a baffled lot." From day one, with the first step, AA creates the false crisis of helplessness. Step 2 confirms alcoholics' "insanity" because the problem that centers in their mind is beyond human remedy. They're helpless, hopeless—in short, powerless. So, constant vigilance and Higher Powers are needed to maintain tentative, one-day-at-a-time sobriety. Recovery means AA, and AA means prayer, meetings, sponsors, and relapses—forever.

It's time to shatter more myths.

No More Recovery—No More Relapse

You are not diseased and you are not powerless; you have no reason to be "in recovery." Starting now, throw out the word *recovery*. Every day is now a *discovery*.

Booze and drugs are yesterday's news. Now, you decide for yourself how you will live your life. No more steps, sponsors or meetings. Discovery means freedom, not only from addiction, but freedom to experience life and live it to the fullest, that is, to live it recovery free.

Since you're not recovering from any disease, "relapse" does not describe using alcohol or other drugs after a period of sobriety. A lapse of judgment and choosing to engage in addictive behavior does describe it. (From here on, use of "relapse" refers to the RGM myth that resuming addictive behavior is due to powerlessness over an addictive disease [alcoholism], which is treatable through Bill Wilson's brand of old-time religion.)

Because of his own disempowering beliefs, Bill W. termed this judgment lapse a "baffling problem, which centers in your mind." You're on your way to discovering that Bill's baffling problem is not so baffling. Nor do you need lifetime AA membership and fellowship with the "baffled lot" to overcome it.

The Myth of Aloneness

"You can't do it alone," is mercilessly driven home in RGM circles. Don't believe it. Don't believe anyone who insists that remaining sober is a lifelong group project. The dismal AA success rate cited in Chapter 1 condemns the RGM's congregational approach. For the RGM, "alone" means anything outside their cloistered walls and limited views.

As well, heightened perception tells us that unless you were stranded by yourself on a desert island, you wouldn't be "alone." By reading this book, and through countless other human contacts and resources, you are not alone. Take advantage of the wealth of information at libraries and on the Internet. Join organizations where people gather with enjoyable like interests. The answers are out there.

The RGM's big lie is that there's only one way to defeat your addiction: "spiritual awakening" (that is, religious conversion) through Bill Wilson's step program. There is no truth in this. It's simply a proselytizing and recruiting tactic.

(Please note that 12-step organizations are *not* self-help groups. Instead, they operate as faith-healing dependency groups. They tell you that without the group your very life is in jeopardy. They want to keep you dependent. But excellent support groups for everything from baldness, to cancer are available. Your concerns, including addictive behaviors, are dealt with constructively, compassionately and sensibly in many of these. Participants do not waste their valuable time, or yours, attempting the spiritual conversions expected of Bill Wilson's followers. Your state's self-help clearing house is a fine resource for finding these self-help support groups. See Appendix B for information on alcohol and drug self-help groups.)

No More Powerlessness

The tremendous fact for every one of us is that we have discovered a common solution. We have a way out on which we can absolutely agree and upon which we can join in brotherly and harmonious action. (The Big Book)

Wilson's followers believe that they are powerless over alcohol. And they are right. They powerlessly band together hoping against hope that their recovery group project will generate the spiritual power needed to overcome their "baffling" compulsion. But their "common solution" is the common problem for millions desperately seeking a way off the recovery merry-go-round.

Bill Wilson's concept of powerlessness is a classic double bind. If you believe his step 1, "We admitted we were powerless over alcohol—that our lives had become unmanageable," and relapse, you demonstrate your powerlessness and inability to manage your affairs. If you don't believe Bill's concept and then drink again, you'll again be "proving" your powerlessness. "See, what more proof do you need? You drank! Admit you are powerless, drop the denial and get with The Program," is the typical AA response to step 1 disbelievers. It's a win-win situation for the RGM, and a lose-lose situation for you. There is only one exception to the double bind: people who don't buy the 12 steps, quit, and never drink again. And even they're dismissed as "dry drunks" by Wilson's "humble" followers.

Let's take it further. When an AA member relapses, this is neatly attributed to his reclaiming his will, which he cannot handle. He has violated AA's first three steps. He has:

1. Taken back his power and attempted to manage his life.
2. Performed an insane act.
3. Reneged on his decision to turn his life and will over to God, as he understood Him.

When he crawls back to meetings, if his shame allows him, he'll be:

1. Greeted with "We told you so" grins (an affirmation of his powerlessness).
2. Given a cup of coffee (sane behavior, as opposed to drinking and trying to manage his life).
3. Joined in dubious contemplation of the baffling problem which centers in his mind. ("Our disease is too much for us. We must turn it over to the One who has all power.")

This relapse-repent-contemplate pattern is a vicious cycle, and is very typical of the recovery merry-go-round. But as long as an errant AA member "continues to take personal inventory, and promptly admits when he is wrong," as step 10 teaches, he'll be "working the program," and thus "in recovery." And for most, "working the program" means relapse, repent and contemplate; relapse, repent and contemplate; relapse, repent and contemplate . . .

The Hazelden Foundation is a major publisher of 12-step "recovery" literature. In one of their books, *The 12 Steps to Happiness*, author Joe Klaas likens powerlessness over alcohol to other instances of powerlessness: a mother presses to her bosom the body of her child run over by a truck; a man crushed under a fallen wall gasps his last breath; a pilot plunges earthward in a burning airliner with 240 passengers. Klaas uses graphic examples of horrific situations that have nothing, absolutely nothing, to do with powerlessness over your own behavior—unless, of course, you believe the myth that an addictive disease has taken over your mind and body, in which case "powerlessness" becomes a self-fulfilling prophecy.

Untold numbers pass through 12-step boot camp where they are indoctrinated to believe that they are "powerless." Even those who can't stand AA often "come to believe" this deadly, self-fulfilling prophecy, and feel crushed, hopeless, because of the Hobson's choice they believe they're faced with: "jails, institutions, or death" or AA meeting after AA meeting after AA meeting—forever. It's little wonder that many drink themselves to death as a result. Those who buy into "the program" fare little better. Relapse-repent-contemplate is the vicious cycle and, worse, because they also believe AA's "one drink, one drunk" self-fulfilling prophecy, their drinking binges often become worse—sometimes far worse—than they were before exposure to AA.

Please don't play the RGM's toxic game; don't buy into its self-fulfilling prophecies. The stakes are too high. You can quit any addiction and live a fulfilling life of discovery. You have the power to do it.

Their Religion is Better Than Yours

Check your religion at the door. Conventional religious beliefs mean nothing to Wilson's recruiters. In AA, everyone is taught that the Higher Powers of their religions aren't powerful enough to foster the miracle of sobriety. Sorry Jesus, Allah and Buddha. And even if a member were to pick Jesus, Allah, or Buddha as their Higher Power, it is only through Alcoholics Anonymous that that Power is supplied. (Clergy must be a particularly tough crowd to convert, as the RGM has specialized rehabs and AA groups just for them.)

An excerpt from the Big Book reveals all. Dr. Carl Jung tells an alcoholic patient:

"You have the mind of a chronic alcoholic. I have never seen one single case recover, where that state of mind existed to the extent that it does in you." Our friend felt as though the gates of hell had closed on him with a clang.

He said to the doctor, "Is there no exception?"

"Yes," replied the doctor, "there is. Exceptions to cases such as yours have been occurring since early times. Here and there, once in a while, alcoholics have had what are called vital spiritual experiences."

Upon hearing this our friend was somewhat relieved, for he reflected that, after all, he was a good church member. This hope, however, was destroyed by the doctor's telling him that *while his religious convictions were very good, in his case they did not spell the necessary vital spiritual experience.* (Italics added)

The Big Book's citation of Jung's comments makes it clear that only the Wilson religion will do; only it will provide "the necessary vital spiritual experience."

Discovery of Self-Acceptance

People addicted to alcohol and other drugs behave deplorably at times. You know you've lied; did you also cheat or steal? How about infidelity or potentially dangerous sexual escapades? Have you been told you're an embarrassment to yourself, family and friends? Were there humiliating social fiascos and embarrassing moments at home, school, or work? Was there trouble with the law? Has your drunken and/or chemically induced behavior hurt those you love and care about the most?

It's not surprising that addictive behaviors culminate in feelings of worthlessness and guilt. In addition, you're looked upon as an insensitive, selfish, irresponsible, lout. Insensitive! Selfish! Irresponsible! A lout! Have you ever heard such words used to describe someone suffering from diabetes, Alzheimer's Disease, kidney failure, or cancer?

I can hear you now, "If I'm not diseased, then I must be an insensitive, selfish, irresponsible lout." Don't panic. Everyone exhibits loutish behavior at one time or another. That's the point. Your addictive behavior was vile; *you* are not. Do you honestly believe that you would have done all those things you're beating yourself up over if you were not under the influence?

Stop beating yourself up. While being loaded is not an excuse, it is the reality behind your lousy behavior. In other words, you, like everyone else, are a fallible human being. You chose to drink, and sometimes you drank too much. That doesn't make you an evil, brain-diseased, spiritual miscreant in need of the RGM's spiritual lube job. It shows that you aren't perfect, and it's in keeping with your human fallibility.

If you're like most people, you'll forgive others their failings. Why not forgive yourself? You can, you know. And it's much better than loathing yourself over behavior that you have wisely decided to change.

We are all imperfect. Your "bad" behavior as an addicted person does not make *you* bad. And feeling guilty won't do you or anyone else any good. Do yourself and others a favor: do your best to accept yourself unconditionally and get on with the tasks at hand—it'll be easier if you aren't weighed down with guilt.

Disempowering feelings of shame or guilt are never in your best interest, and they're worse than useless as motivational fuel for lasting sobriety. The RGM, however, exploits them; the RGM wants to keep you tied forever to the emotional wreckage of your past— wreckage that requires the RGM's Wilsonian spiritual rewiring to patch up.

Accepting yourself unconditionally is the natural state of things. You can choose to do it, and you can do it right now. As an old television commercial said, "Try it, you'll like it." And while you're trying new things, let's make another empowering move.

Self-Worth vs. Self-Esteem

Break free from the crippling concept of self-esteem as taught in RGM circles and throughout our culture. Consider psychologist Albert Ellis's take on this:

> Self-esteem is essentially a rating game and basically means that I am okay as a person if, and only if, I perform well and win the approval of significant others. At first, that sounds great, because if I push myself to achieve and to please others, I will presumably keep feeling good about myself and have high "self-esteem." Hogwash!

The equation for self-esteem reads:

Do well + please others + please self = high self-esteem

Conversely:

Don't do well + displease others + displease self = low self-esteem

Low self-esteem is cited as the cause for such personal and social ills as addiction, child abuse, emotional disturbance, cultism, criminality, and both under and over achievement. Supposedly, people with high self-esteem will not be prone to the personal difficulties and social ills exhibited by those with low self-esteem. But in their book, *The Social Importance of Self-Esteem*, Neil J. Smelser, University Professor of Sociology at the University of California, Berkeley and

Andrew M. Mecca, Executive Director of the California Health Research Foundation report very different results.

> The news is that the associations between self-esteem and its expected consequences are mixed, insignificant, or absent. This nonrelationship holds between self-esteem and teenage pregnancy, self-esteem and child abuse, self-esteem and most cases of alcohol and drug abuse.

Smelser and Mecca did not find substantial evidence linking self-esteem and negative, risky, or self-defeating behaviors. Beware of anyone claiming that treatment is required for your "addiction-breeding low self-esteem." That, as Ellis would say, is hogwash.

Self-esteem means, "If I do well, I feel good. If I do poorly, I feel bad." In other words, it's a form of self-rating. Sure, it's great to knock in the winning run with two out in the bottom of the ninth, but if you buy into self-esteem and you strike out, you're a failure. "Peanuts" cartoonist Charles Schulz capitalized on this to win sympathy for his alter ego, Charlie Brown. If Charlie got the hit, he was the hero. If he didn't, he was the goat. Hitless Charlie Brown saw himself as a downtrodden nobody. But you don't have to see yourself that way. You can *choose* not to play that game.

You're never going to please yourself and others all the time. Throw out the conditional concept of self-esteem and replace it with the unconditional reality of self-acceptance.

Self-acceptance means, "Whether I do well or not, whether I get the hit or not, I can still accept myself as an intrinsically worthwhile human being." Give this gift to yourself; no one can take it away from you. You'll put less pressure on yourself, less pressure on others (you won't be dependent on their opinions of you), and in all likelihood more pleasant to be around and happier. Your self-worth, that is, your intrinsic worthiness as a self-accepting, unique individual, takes precedence over the RGM's self-esteem rating games.

Being Sorry Without Being Foolish

What about the people you mistreated while living under the fog of alcohol and other drugs. Should you chalk it up to human fallibility and forget it? Unlike AA's eighth and ninth steps which speak of making amends as part of their formula for your twelfth step epiphany, wouldn't you agree that it's simply the decent thing to apologize to anyone you've harmed, anytime? Set the record straight. Make your apologies. Say, "I'm sorry" (if you mean it); do everything possible, but sensible in the name of reparation.

Sensible? Here's a tip. Only own up to family and friends, at least for now. Confession may be good for the soul, but employers and law enforcement officials might see it another way. You could find yourself out of work or behind bars. Don't let the AA slogan, "We're only as sick as our secrets" trouble you. You're not sick, the slogan is. It's just another excuse for relapsing, blamed on "secrets" you haven't revealed. There's no need to grovel for anyone's forgiveness. Return money or property anonymously if you choose. Confess when you feel the time is right, if at all. Foolishness isn't part of the "discovery" package. And don't expect everyone to accept your apologies. Some people are slow to forgive; others may never do it. Time and sobriety are your best allies. But understand—sobriety is not contingent on making amends or the forgiveness of others. While both are good, neither is required.

Self-acceptance is not a concession to the status quo. On the contrary, self-acceptance is your green light to discovery. With it, your adventures begin starting with your mastery over addiction. Without it, the weight of your drinking past will leave you guilty and frustrated. As Admiral David Farragut said, "Damn the torpedoes, full speed ahead." Or, for our purpose, "Damn these human fallibilities, discoveries lie ahead."

AA's Slant

Unconditional acceptance of self and others, (since you're fallible, so is everyone else—but of course you have the right to defend yourself) isn't far from AA's Serenity Prayer:

God, grant me the Serenity to accept the things I cannot change, Courage to change the things I can, and Wisdom to know the difference.

Bill W. liked The Serenity Prayer, and AA adopted it in 1939. The following excerpt is from the January 1950 AA publication, *The Grapevine:*

The timeless little prayer has been credited to almost every theologian, philosopher and saint known to man. The most popular opinion on its authorship favors St. Francis of Assisi. It was actually written by Dr. Reinhold Niebuhr, of the Union Theological Seminary, NYC, in about 1932 as the ending to a longer prayer. It came to the attention of an early member of AA in 1939. He liked it so much he brought it to Bill W. Bill and the staff read the prayer and felt that it particularly suited the needs of AA. Cards were printed and passed around. Thus, the simple little prayer became an integral part of the AA movement.

Self-acceptance, acceptance of others, and the courage to change are not unique to the RGM. What is unique in the RGM is that all of these things depend on practicing the "divinely inspired" teachings of Bill W. (Indeed, many AA members believe that the Big Book is God's word penned through an inspired Bill Wilson.) So, in AA, all of these things are conditional.

Untold volumes have been written concerning the existence or nonexistence of God. Friends, these topics and God's role (if any) in granting serenity are for another day and another book. As we noted earlier, these subjects are irrelevant to ending addictive behavior and are more suited to Bible study and Sunday school. As part of your newfound freedom from addiction and RGM tyranny, spiritual and religious concepts will be yours for the taking, or not, when you want, with whom you want. Contrary to ATI and RGM edicts, blending God and religion into the getting-and-staying-sober mix is *not* necessary.

Why Are You Quitting?

Why do you want to quit drinking or taking drugs? Is it for a dose of high self-esteem? Do you want to be a "winner," as in the AA slogan, "Stick with the winners"? It's a risky proposition. "Winners" are compliant AA members, tentatively sober, and temporarily enjoying their conditional dose of high self-esteem. Guess what happens when their self-esteem goes into the toilet, as it inevitably will, eventually.

AA labels people, not their behavior. Even when your behavior is the result of their mythical disease, you, as an "alcoholic," are bad. Joining AA's recovery fellowship puts you on the road to becoming good: a grateful, recovering alcoholic or addict. In lieu of using the labels "bad," and "good," AA calls you "sick," and then, by becoming one of them, you get "well." It's as if AA has cornered the market on wellness and betterment. (Go to any AA meeting and judge for yourself how "well" those in attendance are.)

Recovery intends to make sick people "well" (that is, in conscious contact with God and leading a God-controlled life). But nothing in the 12 steps of Alcoholics Anonymous addresses how to quit drinking or how to end life-destroying addictions. What the 12 steps do contain, in fact, what they consist of, is a blueprint for religious conversion, complete with ego deflation, prayer, abandonment of self-direction, and a plentiful helping of moralism. You must be bad, so they can make you good.

But quitting booze or drugs doesn't make bad people good or losers into winners. It doesn't make anyone "better than well." It makes fallible people wiser, happier, and capable of doing bigger and better things. That's all. And it's enough.

There's nothing wrong with wanting to better yourself and enrich your life. Quitting booze and/or drugs is a great way to begin. Getting religion can be great too, when you choose it freely. But there is something very wrong when, under the guise of treatment and altruism, the ATI and RGM dupe unsuspecting people into believing that sobriety and betterment can only be achieved through Alcoholics Anonymous and its program of religious conversion. There's nothing "spiritual" about adopting religious beliefs out of fear and desperation.

It's clear: The RGM needs you much more than you need the RGM. In fact, you don't need the recovery group movement at all.

So, why do you want to quit drinking or taking other drugs? There's no need for deep introspection. As noted in Chapter 4, if drinking is causing more pain than pleasure, it's time to quit. As noted in Chapter 5, if the service alcohol once provided in relaxing and socializing has developed into a disservice, it's time to quit. And, as you'll find, things do get better as you discover a fascinating (not perfect) new world previously hidden under a chemically induced haze.

In the Beginning

Why were you drinking or using drugs in the first place? There are as many "reasons" as there are people drinking and using. Addiction therapists will have you unearthing "addiction breeding" childhood events and memories: acne; a bad haircut or perm; being overweight or skinny; being overprotected; being tall or short; being the youngest, middle, oldest or only child; being unsupervised; being shy; being gregarious; being emotionally, physically, or sexually abused; the death of a relative or pet; homosexuality; no prom date; parents' divorce; striking out in the big game; the bicycle that was never under the Christmas tree; the dress you didn't get on your tenth birthday; wearing hand-me-downs; or wearing glasses. I'm not kidding about any of this; virtually any childhood experience can be blamed for your descent into alcoholism and addiction.

Good memories are part of a romanticized childhood you can never return to. And your bad memories are just plain bad. They're dead. They're in the past. And they certainly have nothing to do with why you're drinking (or not) now, as you'll see shortly.

The Victim

The "inner child" movement was popularized by such 12-stepping new-age gurus as John Bradshaw. "Healing the wounded inner-child" will supposedly free you from the emotional bondage that fuels your addictive behaviors. Bradshaw's message is clear: you're the innocent victim of outside forces. Your childhood wounds manifest themselves in adult addictive behaviors. So now you live unmanageable lives as powerless drunks and addicts. What the inner-child movement doesn't get, or cannot accept, is that no matter what befell someone, addiction is a *choice*. Happiness is a choice, too, that requires effort at times. You're an adult, now. You'll continue to be a "victim" of childhood trauma only if you choose to be.

Enjoying life with child-like wonder is one thing, but it's time the inner-child grew up. Lincoln put it this way: "People are just as happy as they make up their minds to be." Don't fall into the "I'm a victim" mentality. To use the current jargon, it's "disempowering"— and it will lead you straight into the powerlessness trap.

You Liked It Too Much

Let's cut to the chase. People drink and use because they like the pleasurable effects—and they like them a lot. Even the Big Book gets this right. In "The Doctor's Opinion" section, William G. Silkworth, M.D., states, "Men and women drink essentially because they like the effect produced by alcohol."

To put this in personal terms, think of the reasons why you drank. Take the time to really think. Got it? Good. You drank because you were happy; you drank because you were sad; you drank because you were nervous; and you drank when you wanted to unwind or just hang out with the gang. Now think of when you drank. If you're like most of us, you drank when there were tears and you drank when there were smiles. What all of this has in common is that you sought the pleasurable effect of alcohol. And you're about to master that pleasure drive for good, without treatment or recovery. The RGM doesn't want you to know that you can do this. But you can.

What Was, Was

"Closure" is an all-consuming buzzword. Past issues must be resolved, no matter what the cost. Unless you achieve closure, "what was" will supposedly haunt you. Therefore "closure" is required for the "recovering" crowd. They spend their time dwelling, analyzing, and resolving rather than learning, loving, and living. But closure is not required for sobriety or happiness.

In *The Codependency Conspiracy*, authors Stan J. Katz and Aimee I. Liu offer their impressions of dwelling in the past:

> It's a bit like trying to drive a car while looking only in the rear view mirror. You don't get very far that way, and you run the risk of a crack-up. I prefer to check the rear view from time to time, making sure that the reflection is accurate, but concentrate most of my attention on the road ahead. Only if I see something gaining on me from behind do I stop to deal with it.

You are not helplessly tied to unresolved past events. People who feel that they are tied to their pasts, people desperate for "closure," seem to find themselves on psychiatrists' couches or guest starring on Jerry Springer and Ricki Lake. While we all want to see how the movie ends, write your own finish if you don't know the last scene. You can do this. You can write your own ending. Try it. Of course, "close" what you can, but when you can't, it's time to move on. Learn from the past, live in the present, and keep an eye toward the future.

Discovery of Pain/Pleasure

Almost all human behavior, even the simplest everyday action, is directed in one way: to avoid pain and seek pleasure. Alcohol/drug abusers know their booze and drugs are not working for them any longer. Still, the pleasures they associate with them over-ride the current pain caused by their drinking/using. This is the nature of any addiction: to engage repeatedly in pain-causing behaviors despite knowing the severe negative consequences of those behaviors. The RGM attributes this to a disease, over which you are powerless. But we know better.

It's a simple matter of pain, pleasure, and selective memory: alcoholics/addicts tend to concentrate on their positive experiences with alcohol or other drugs, and to minimize the negative experiences. But eventually the negative experiences become too numerous and too painful to ignore any longer. It's usually a long, painful time coming. But with heightened perception you're there now. As motion picture legend Peter O'Toole observed, an alcohol buzz is "a fifteen minute glow followed by three days of hell." For O'Toole, the pain (finally) outweighed the pleasure.

In the next chapter you'll address and master your self-defeating pleasure drive gone awry.

Chapter 9

Minding Your Minds:
Your Two Ways of Thinking

"It is not enough to have a good mind; the main thing is to use it."
—Rene Descartes

Addiction "experts" vary greatly as to what comprises their "incurable, progressive disease." They define it, variously, as a brain disease, developmental deficit, distorted coping mechanism, neurochemical imbalance, genetic predisposition, symptom of family dysfunction or the environment, learned behavior, or combinations thereof. No matter what science determines, Bill Wilson's program springs eternal as the sole antidote. One thing Bill got half-right though: it's a "baffling problem that centers in your mind." Only it's not so baffling once you discover your power over it.

When the American Medical Association accepted the disease concept of alcoholism in 1956 (it's not a scientific "theory"; it's merely a weak hypothesis), it opened the floodgates for "treatment." Those gates opened wide in 1970 when the Hughes Act created the National Institute on Alcohol Abuse and Alcoholism and mandated that insurance companies foot the bill for treatment. As a result, the treatment industry sprang up in mushroom-like fashion, as it was watered with a river of government and insurance-industry cash.

During their heyday in the 1980s, private rehabs commanded hefty fees for a typical 28-day stay. Thirty thousand dollars and up was common, as were multiple stays. Today, insurance companies are (at least in part) wise to the addiction treatment industry's get-rich-quick scheme. They see dismal recovery rates and have severely reduced monies for what they now know is fundamentally ineffective treatment. In a desperate bid to recoup their loses, rehab operators switched to less costly, high-profit outpatient treatment, which is essentially group therapy run by Bill Wilson groupies who have secured alcohol/drug counselor certification.

But a more disturbing trend has developed: rehabs are now routinely admitting their clients as Mentally Ill Chemical Abusers. MICA is the diagnosis *du jour*. This dual diagnosis gives ATI professionals "genuine" psychiatric disorders to bill for and treat, in addition to the "disease" of alcoholism. Is it coincidence that all these "real" psychiatric problems were not diagnosed back when insurance companies were blindly doling out megabucks for alcohol and drug treatment alone? Whether or not you have a MICA diagnosis, your "treatment" still boils down to a life sentence of addictive disease within the barless prison cell of never-ending 12-step recovery.

Be wary of this insurance dollar-motivated MICA misdiagnosis. The last thing you need is the addiction treatment industry attaching yet another label to you. [1]

The "Baffling Problem"

Robert Downey Jr. and baseball's Darryl Strawberry are two of the ATI's poster boys. Both have been "recovering" for years and are sad testimony to the relapse-repent-contemplate cycle of the recovery merry-go-round. Their highly publicized relapses are always blamed on the insidiousness of addictive disease and their failure to live by AA's spiritual teachings. A much more accurate read on their relapses would be garbage in (12-step treatment), garbage out (relapses).

Robert and Darryl are tragic examples of Bill Wilson's "baffling problem." Since their Higher Powers have yet to save them, their baffling problem runs amok, causing repeated relapses. Instead of teaching them how to overcome their addictions, Merry-Go-Round operators quote the Big Book: "Rarely have we seen a person fail who has thoroughly followed our path." In the minds of operators, it's clear: Robert and Darryl aren't following The Program—they need more "treatment." We now know from Chapter 8 how a relapse vio-

---

1. Addiction therapists want to analyze your emotional/psychological disturbances. By dint of mastering one's addictive behavior, these disturbances typically fade and emotional stability and general well-being usually follow within a few weeks of stopping drinking/drugging. But remember, alcohol is a depressant, which could affect your mood longer than a few weeks. Like everyone else who quits, you'll have challenges to meet. Maximize your chances by having a clear head. If, after a few weeks, melancholy or depression persist, it may make sense to seek professional/medical advice for your blues, *not* for addiction treatment.

lates AA's first three steps. So, "treatment" continues with counselors focusing on where Robert and Darryl went wrong with the remaining steps:

Step 4. Made a searching and fearless moral inventory of ourselves.
(Counselor: "Robert and Darryl's moral assessments weren't thorough and/or weren't compiled fearlessly enough.")

Step 5. Admitted to God, to ourselves and to another human being, the exact nature of our wrongs.
(Counselor: "Robert and Darryl don't know the exact nature of their wrongs, and/or haven't declared them to God, themselves and someone else. It's also possible that they know their wrongs, but haven't admitted them, or refuse to admit them.")

Step 6. Were entirely ready to have God remove all these defects of character.
(Counselor: "Robert and Darryl weren't totally ready for God's intervention, which paradoxically is a character defect itself.)

Step 7. Humbly asked Him to remove our shortcomings.
(Counselor: "Robert and Darryl haven't petitioned God with appropriate humility.")

Step 8. Made a list of all persons we had harmed and became willing to make amends to them all.
(Counselor: "Robert and Darryl didn't list everyone they hurt, and/or were not willing to make restitution.")

Step 9. Made direct amends to such people wherever possible, except when to do so would inure them or others.
(Counselor: "Robert and Darryl haven't made their peace with those they harmed and/or hurt someone in their attempts.")

Step 10. Continued to take personal inventory and when we were wrong promptly admitted it.
(Counselor: "Robert and Darryl haven't continued taking stock of their moral failings and/or did not promptly admit their wrongs.")

Step 11. Sought through prayer and meditation to improve our conscious contact with God as we understood Him, praying only for knowledge of His will for us and the power to carry that out.
(Counselor: "Robert and Darryl haven't prayed and/or meditated enough. This leaves them lacking in conscious contact with the One who provides knowledge and power.")

Step 12. Having had a spiritual awakening as the result of these steps, we tried to carry this message to alcoholics, and to practice these principles in all our affairs.
(Counselor: "Robert and Darryl must continue working the steps where a spiritual awakening awaits. This relieves their 'baffling mind problem' allowing them to spread the AA word and live by Bill Wilson's divinely inspired doctrine.")

Robert's and Darryl's ill fates are entirely in keeping with their addiction treatment/recovery group experiences. Deceived, they believe themselves to be powerless victims of an incurable disease. Hence, they are "powerless" over their relapses. And Robert and Darryl "prove" this repeatedly. Also, please note that *all* blame for their relapses is placed directly on Robert and Darryl; this is in keeping with the RGM article of faith that the 12-step program is perfect, that it *always* "works if you work it." Needless to say, this is the handiest excuse imaginable for treatment failures.

The bottom line is that we do not have to share Robert's and Darryl's ongoing tragedy. We can do for ourselves that which the RGM insists cannot be done—independently quit booze and drugs for good. Read what addiction researcher and author Stanton Peele, Ph.D. says in the book, *Coming Clean—Overcoming Addiction Without Treatment*:

> [A]sk any 12-step counselor or group member what the hardest addiction is to quit. Inevitably, the person will indicate smoking. Then ask the person if he or she or a family member ever smoked and quit. If so, ask how he or she or the family member accomplished this—only one person in twenty will say it was due to therapy or a support group. Muse with this person over how, while believing all addiction requires treatment and group assistance to overcome, this person or those closest to him or her beat the hardest addiction on their own.

Even the Director of the National Institute on Alcohol Abuse and Alcoholism, Enoch Gordis, acknowledges treatment's shaky foundation:

> In the case of alcoholism, our whole treatment system, with its innumerable therapies, armies of therapists, large and expensive programs, endless conferences and public relations activities is founded on hunch, not evidence, and not on science.

The self-discovered know the secret to Bill Wilson's "baffling problem." In fact, the "secret" used by millions has been known for ages—since long before Bill and his followers began their "non-religious" recovery movement. Despite the RGM's well-orchestrated efforts to convince us otherwise, science is bearing out what many of us know intuitively: we carry within us the power to quit our addictions for good. The science behind Wilson's "baffling problem" begins and ends with you.

Thinking about booze continues after corking the bottle. Just because you have quit doesn't mean that your addiction has quit (yet). Bill Wilson knew this. But his baffled mind told him he was powerless over it. Baffled Bill and his RGM automatons may be powerless—but you are not.

The secret to overcoming Bill's baffling problem is that you are, at least metaphorically, functioning with two minds: Rational and Emotional. In his best selling book *Emotional Intelligence*, Daniel Goleman, Ph.D., explains our dual minds:

> These two fundamentally different ways of knowing interact to construct our mental life. One, the rational mind, is the mode of comprehension we are typically conscious of: more prominent in awareness, thoughtful, able to ponder and reflect. But alongside that there is another system of knowing: impulsive and powerful, if sometimes illogical-the emotional mind. . . .
>
> These two minds, the emotional and the rational, operate in tight harmony for the most part. Ordinarily there is a balance between emotional and rational minds, with emotion feeding into and informing the operations of the rational mind, and the rational mind refining and sometimes vetoing the inputs of emotions.
>
> In many or most moments these minds are exquisitely coordinated; feelings are essential to thought, thought to feeling. But when passions surge the balance tips: it is the emotional mind that captures the upper hand, swamping the rational mind.

Addictive behavior is one of many behaviors spurred by the emotional mind. "Tonight Show" host, Jay Leno, hit on this when he asked actor Hugh Grant, "What were you thinking" in reference to Hugh's tryst with a prostitute. We all know what Hugh was thinking, and it wasn't about the consequences of his behavior. Hugh's emotional mind had the upper hand, which led to his actions.

Think of your own experiences. Have you ever asked yourself,

"What did I do that for?" This question comes from your rational mind, after you did something you regret. You acted on emotions, which swamped your rational mind. To your advantage, the emotional mind instantly removes your hand from a hot stove. It allows the baseball player to stab a line drive. These reactions are performed without conscious thought. It's pure reaction to external cues. But you don't have to react (the way you have) to addiction cues, be they external or internal. You can learn to recognize and reject the cues and those unwanted messages that spawn addictive behavior.

The Dual Mind Cycle of Addiction

A basic understanding of the brain solves a big part of Bill W.'s baffling problem. Daniel Goleman explains:

> The most primitive part of the brain . . . [root brain] regulates basic life functions like breathing . . . This primitive brain cannot be said to think or learn; rather it is a set of preprogrammed regulators that keep the body running as it should and reacting in a way that ensures survival.
>
> Millions of years later in evolution, from these emotional areas evolved the thinking brain or neocortex. The fact that the thinking brain grew from the emotional reveals much about the relationship of thought to feeling; there was an emotional brain long before there was a rational one.
>
> With the arrival of the first mammals came new, key layers of the emotional brain . . . called the "limbic" system . . . When we are in the grip of craving or fury, head-over-heels in love or recoiling in dread, it is the limbic system that his us in its grip.

Your rational brain knows you don't need booze/drugs for survival, but your emotional brain doesn't. Couple this with the pleasure booze/drugs provide and the emotional brain becomes fiercely protective of your addictions in the same manner it protects your sex drive. The emotional brain places addictions in the "necessary for survival" category.

The self-discovered recognize the "emotional mind's" attempt to control their behavior. In the spirit of self-interest, they've learned how to veto its unprincipled inputs as a matter of choice, not will power. You will too.

There has been endless speculation on the physical mechanisms of addiction. Thus far, very little can be said with certainty in this area.

The Dual-Mind Cycle of Addiction

3. Rational Mind
Swamped with craving messages, the urge "must" be satisfied. Filters out the negative consequences of past abuse. Focuses on the pleasure.

2. Emotional Mind
Interprets the messages as a craving/urge arousing pleasurable memories of the effects of alcohol or other drugs.

4. Rational Brain
Verbalizes addiction, survival, craving and pleasure messages:
"Gotta have it."
"I want it."
"Time for a drink."
"I need it."

1. Emotional Brain
Sends out survival, addiction and pleasure messages. The cycle begins.

5. The Result
You reach for the booze or other drugs and drink, take, shoot, snort, smoke . . .

6. Resolution
Relief and pleasure. The cycle is complete and the addiction is temporarily satisfied.

The cycle that you will overcome!

And for our purposes, physical mechanisms, causes, or contributory factors are largely beside the point—which is sobering up—because people overcome addictions every day without a clue as to the physical mechanisms involved. Nor do those mechanisms make any difference to them. You're not a slave to biological signals from underfed addictions. Cravings won't kill you; using alcohol and other drugs to relieve cravings might.

Yes, you will be uncomfortable from time to time. Just remember that this is temporary and will get better with time until you'll reach the point (which you will) where the discomfort is just a bad memory.

The dual-mind cycle of addiction then, offers you a way to visualize and think about the cycle of addictive behavior. Described in physical terms, the dual mind cycle is an aid to help you help yourself break the cycle of your destructive addictive behavior. See the above figure for a visual aid.

Alcoholics drink because they seek pleasurable effects from booze; and for many, drinking is an immediate way of temporarily avoiding emotional pain—never mind the emotional and physical pain that comes later. Your emotional mind interprets "later" as "never," and when you think of booze the emotional mind's selective memory kicks in and, normally, you'll concentrate on your positive feelings.

Here's the cycle: The emotional brain sends out addiction survival messages and emotional brain pleasure centers light up. The emotional mind interprets this as a craving and wants you to act on the urge, just as it wants you to gasp for air after holding your breath, or gobble food when hungry. Now, the rational mind becomes swamped with craving messages you "must" satisfy. Negative aspects of your boozing past become secondary to the hoped-for chemical gratification gained by drinking. At this moment, the rational brain surrenders and you say: "I want it," "I need it," "Gotta have it." Physiologically, increased heart rate and adrenaline rushes often occur. You want to avoid pain and gain pleasure, so you reach for the booze or other drugs. That in itself often calms the urge. But taking the drink or drug satisfies the urge and quiets the brain. Temporarily. When the emotional brain again interprets the addiction as threatened, the cycle begins once more.

Often, when the emotional mind wants immediate relief from emotional pain, the cycle kicks in again. Ironically, this attempt to relieve pain causes more pain (both physical and emotional), leading to a further desire to relieve pain through drinking, which causes more pain, etc., etc., etc. And the beat goes on; the cycle continues. Contemplating the soothing effects of a drink/drug, any withdrawal symptom, or the thought that your alcohol/drug supply is in danger, is enough to spur the cycle. You've seen this at the local tavern when "Last call for alcohol!" sparks a drinking frenzy and the buying of packaged goods.

This is the cycle of addictive behavior: the dual-mind cycle of addiction, a cycle you will break without treatment. While it may a problem for you now, it will not be a lifelong, "baffling problem."

Nicotine gum and patch manufactures know the dual-mind cycle of addiction well. Their products deliver nicotine, which quiets a smoker's brain messages to, "light up," just as a drink or two quiets the boozer's "time for a drink" message. After withdrawal, ex-smokers still face brain messages, which ultimately demand, "time to light-up again." Indeed, all former addicts face the "give me what I crave" quandary. For the self-discovered, these post-withdrawal demands become post-addiction whimpers.

The dual-mind cycle explains Bill Wilson's "baffling problem, which centers in your mind." If Robert Downey and Darryl Strawberry (along with countless others) were empowered instead of indoctrinated with false and sometimes death-dealing notions of addictive disease and supernatural remedies, the learned powerlessness they bought into would become a thing of the past.

Understanding the dual-mind cycle doesn't insure the end of addiction. It does take the mystery out of it and paves the way for mastering it. You now have discovered that addictive thoughts, "I want it," "I need It," stem from primitive emotional desires for survival of the addiction and to avoid pain and to gain pleasure.

Whenever you feel the desire to drink/use, whenever you think of engaging in behaviors you have wisely decided to stop or change, identify those feelings/thoughts as the enemy within. This enemy's singular mission is to convince you to seek out and ingest some intoxicant to satisfy its primal urges. Addiction has become the master ordering you to fetch. You're about to reclaim your power and become master once again, as you order addiction to heel.

Thinking and Emotions

As stated in Chapter 4, "To change your feelings/emotions, change your thinking." You may now be questioning that statement. The dual-mind cycle of addiction posits that the emotional brain influences and sometimes overwhelms the thinking brain. We can, however, learn to keep our rational (that is, self-preserving) mind in charge. To do this, it's helpful to understand how our thinking helps to create our emotions.

Take, for example, the terrorist attack on New York City's World Trade Center. We feel emotional about the attack because we think of how evil it was, and how much so many innocent people suffered. We think of the unfortunate souls trapped in the crumbling edifice as we imagine their terror. Our hearts bleed for the skyjacked airline passengers as we think of their ill-fated flights. We think of the heroic police officers and fire fighters crushed to death while trying to save others. We feel for the grief-stricken families who lost loved ones as we think of their sorrow. Here, our thinking creates our emotions. We think about the attack, (if only for seconds) and form our appraisal, which elicits the emotions of shock, anger, sadness, grief, loss, and horror.

On the other hand, pain-avoidance and pleasure drives are "programmed" into your emotional makeup. The potential for addiction exists whether you stir primal passions with alcohol, other drugs, sex, food, computers or gambling. Your emotional side is going to protect the addiction as if your life depends on it. It doesn't.

Use Your Minds Well

This chapter began with a quote from Descartes, "It is not enough to have a good mind; the main thing is to use it well." That's my desire for you—to use your mind(s) well. I have confidence in your ability to quit booze and drugs now, permanently. While I cannot teach you motivation, I can provide facts and information that will empower and, I hope, inspire you. The power at your command for living alcohol and drug free, on your terms, is limitless.

Henry Ford said: "Thinking is the hardest work there is, which is probably the reason so few engage in it."

All along I've spoken about heightened perception—your intuitive or learned skill to see situations realistically and to think things through. Use it! It's your ticket to freedom. The easily understood dual-mind cycle of addiction is one of many discoveries leading to that freedom—including freedom from a subcultural existence as a recovering Wilsonite. Let your own HP—your heightened perception—guide you to freedom from addiction *and* from the recovery group movement.

By now you're aware that addiction (alcoholism) is not the unconquerable disease of brain-baffled Bill Wilson and the addiction treatment industry. It's a *choice*. In the next chapter, you'll master your addictive behaviors and put this unfortunate part of your life behind you.

Chapter 10

The Parasite

"They always say time changes things, but you actually have
to change them yourself."
—Andy Warhol

Hitting Recovery Bottom

Have you hit bottom yet? According to the recovery group movement's spiritual hucksters, you need to hit bottom for Bill Wilson's magical "miracle" to materialize. What's more, instructions for AA recruitment of the most vulnerable (those who have "hit bottom") as well as for infiltrating their families and securing personal information are found in the Big Book chapter innocently called "Working With Others":

When you discover a prospect for Alcoholics Anonymous, find out all you can about him. . . .
[H]ave a good talk with the person most interested in him, usually his wife. Get an idea of his behavior, his problems, his background, the seriousness of his condition and his religious leanings. You need this information to put yourself in his place, to see how you would like him to approach you if the tables were turned. . . .
Sometimes it is wise to wait till he goes on a binge. Wait for the end of the spree, or at least for a lucid interval. . . .
When your man is better, the doctor might suggest a visit from you. Though you have talked with the family, leave them out of the first discussion. Under these conditions your prospect will see he is under no pressure. Call on him while he is still jittery. He may be more receptive when depressed.

"Hitting bottom" is an RGM term. It defines utter helplessness and hopelessness, when alternatives seem exhausted and "recovery" is the only option. Feeling isolated, guilty, fearful and angry with themselves, vulnerable newcomers feel a sense of belonging when they meet with similarly suffering others. However, this sense of belonging quickly develops into a form of psychological bondage, and later (after the "pink cloud") into a pervasive sense of dread as AA disciples spew their ominous predictions that without them it's jails, institutions or death. But there's a payoff for your devotion to almighty Bill and his Program. It's called The Promises:

> We are going to know a new freedom and new happiness. We will not regret the past or wish to shut the door on it. We will comprehend the word serenity and we will know peace. No matter how far down the scale we have gone, we will see how our experience can benefit others. That feeling of uselessness and self-pity will disappear. We will lose interest in selfish things and gain interest in our fellows. Self seeking will slip away. Our whole attitude and outlook upon life will change. Fear of people and of economic insecurity will leave us. We will intuitively know how to handle situations which used to baffle us. We will suddenly realize that God is doing for us what we could not do for ourselves. (The Big Book)

Sounds like a pretty good payoff doesn't it? Give yourself body, mind and soul to them, and you'll have just about everything you ever wanted. Not just sobriety, but a life steeped in spiritual wonder, personal bliss, and economic security. But there is one catch: If you ever leave them, a crack in the sidewalk will look like the tumbling walls of Jericho and "Your misery will be refunded." (The Big Book)

You don't have to sell your soul to experience The Promises. Pacts with the devil always seem to end with the soul seller desperately trying to back out of the contract. The twist with AA is that they will let you out of the deal, but you're still going to burn in hell for it through "jails, institutions, or death."

Let's stop this day-in-day-out madness, relentlessly promoted by the RGM and ATI. No more devils and demons, no more ambiguous higher powers and disempowering self-labels, no more steps, sponsors, slogans, Bill babble or fictional diseases, and no more dire threats.

Let's end your addiction. Rather, you can end your addiction and rejoin society as a self-discovered person who simply does not drink (drug, gamble, smoke, overeat, etc.) any longer. It's time to take moral and personal responsibility to quit booze and other drugs. Addictions are of your own doing; ending them will be of your own doing, too. In other words, you got yourself into this, and you can get yourself out.

The term "hitting bottom" makes some sense, though, in certain circumstances. It does describe people already "in recovery" who feel isolated, guilty, fearful, and angry with themselves—people who are wondering whether they're defective, constitutionally incapable of being honest, or even crazy. Call it hitting a "recovery bottom."

This is a good thing. It can lead to the heightened-perception realization that getting out of recovery is the only healthy option. Imagine the sense of relief and belonging (without bondage) felt by those who have hit "recovery bottom" when they discover how many people are already out there successfully sober—and free from their recovery merry-go-round nightmare!

Blurred Vision

Addiction treatment focuses on everything under the sun except teaching you how to end your self-defeating, pleasure-seeking, addictive behavior. All the fluff behind treatment—aftercare, relapse triggers, relapse prevention programs, enablers, codependence, personal powerlessness, higher powers, spiritual awakenings, denial, meetings, sponsors, disease, etc.—gives lots of professional merry-go-round operators lots of work, at your expense. Both personally and financially. America's rehab centers overlook your natural desire for pleasure, which leads to addiction(s). Instead, they exploit your booze-rattled emotions while they "treat" your "chronic relapsing brain disease" with new-age recovery psychobabble and supernatural, faith-healing remedies. People addicted to alcohol or other drugs need to discover how to end their self-defeating behavior, period. If you want to end your addiction/dependence now and for good, do it. Life after booze/drugs will be a discovery, I promise you.

First, Recognize Your Self-Talk

For many years, Tom Selleck starred as Private Investigator Thomas Magnum in the popular TV series "Magnum P.I." Thomas told the audience about the "little voice" he heard in his head. Sometimes a warning, sometimes a gut feeling, it offered him insights and gave him pause to think, which is what heightened perception pushes you to do. While Thomas's little voice was not the emotional plea of an underfed addiction, it does illustrate an important point: We all "hear" voices. We call these voices "self-talk. "

In the language of discovery, self-talk is the "I Gotta have it," "I need it," "I want it" stage of the dual-mind cycle of addiction. Whenever self-talk urges you to drink/use, or engage in behaviors you have wisely decided to stop or change, recall the dual-mind cycle and recognize the self-talk as your rational brain's voicing of the pleas of your addiction-, survival- and pleasure-driven emotional brain. By simply recognizing the self-talk, you're building a solid foundation for defeating it.

Begin now. Identify addiction self-talk as your enemy. Separate yourself from it by branding all addiction self-talk as the voice of a parasitic opportunist, an opportunist that only wants one thing: to persuade you ("Gotta have it," "I want it") to drink. Let's expose this enemy for what it is, your soon to be former nemesis: The Parasite

Second, The Parasite

A parasite is something that feeds on the existence of, and often lives within, another. It draws its strength from, and contributes nothing to the well-being of, the host off which it lives. Self-talk that suggests drinking, using other drugs, or engaging in other addictive behaviors is your Parasite, an enemy within that contributes nothing to the well-being of the host: you. Your Parasite draws its strength by enticing you to act on its behalf. In other words, when *it* says, "Time for a drink," it's *you* that physically gets up off your duff, seeks out some booze or drug, and drinks it, shoots it, snorts it, or smokes it. The Parasite is powerless. You are not. The Parasite needs you to run its boozing errands; you don't need it.

Humans think in words and pictures, and the Parasite is of course a metaphor for your destructive, addictive self-talk. Unlike the recovery group movement's supernatural higher powers and mysterious demons, The Parasite is the symbol for something very real: the language ("Gotta have it," "I want it") of your addiction. The problem is that all too often you obeyed The Parasite. And all too often you got drunk. Let's change that.

Early sobriety is a tenuous time. The Parasite is now "starving." It's not like the days before sobriety when you habitually "fed" The Parasite, thus keeping it relatively calm. When The Parasite said, "Time for a drink," you drank. But now, you no longer act on its slightest request. Before long, the intensity of its pleas for "nourishment" (alcohol, drugs, gambling) will subside because The Parasite grows weaker with every sober day. Throw a monkey wrench into the dual-mind cycle of addiction. Start using your heightened perception to identify The Parasite. By zeroing in on this enemy, you will smother its noxious plan; you'll slowly "starve" it to death.

Third, The Parasite, Again

You're sober, but The Parasite isn't ready to leave you alone. Unlike the physical cravings of withdrawal, The Parasite is an emotional protagonist. It's a shrewd chameleon, "speaking" in your own voice, whispering, bellowing, harrying you to fill its own selfish needs.

Take a moment to recall the deceptive self-talk of your own Parasite. Perhaps you'll recognize some of the following:

"I'll only have three";
"I deserve a little now; after all, it's been two weeks";
"You can have a few tonight; just don't drive";
"You won't have any fun at the game without some beer";
"We can handle it; this time will be different";
"We can sleep it off tomorrow";
"I'm bored, time for a drink";
"I want it, just a few won't hurt";
"I need it."

Sound familiar? Too familiar? Notice that The Parasite's insidious self-talk may be in first, second, or third person, and modulates from subtle to demanding. Recognize this self-talk. Add your own familiar messages to the list and try this: separate yourself from The Parasite and the language that it uses. See how it disguises itself with "I," "You," and "We" statements. Then, by simply using a common cognitive technique called *translation*, unmasking The Parasite becomes easy. Look:

"I won't drink any more than three" becomes
"The Parasite wants me to drink at least three."

"I deserve a little now. After all, it's been two weeks" becomes
"The Parasite wants me to think I deserve a little now and that two weeks is long enough."

"You can have a few tonight; just don't drive" becomes
"The Parasite wants me to have a few tonight." (Notice how The Parasite will add, "Just don't drive," as if it was looking out for your best interests.)

"You won't have any fun at the game without some beer" becomes
"The Parasite won't have any fun without some beer." (Remember, you don't want The Parasite having "fun" at your expense.)

"We can handle it; this time will be different" becomes
"The Parasite wants to handle things; chances are that nothing will be different." ("We" is a Parasite ploy attempting to drag you into the team spirit. There are no teams, only you versus The Parasite.)

"We can sleep it off tomorrow" becomes
"The Parasite wants me to sleep it off tomorrow." (The Parasite will gladly sleep with you anytime, at the expense of all your relationships.)

"I'm bored, time for a drink" becomes
"The Parasite is bored and says it's time for a drink."

"I want it, just a few won't hurt" becomes
"The Parasite wants it, and a few will hurt."

"I need it" becomes
"The Parasite needs it."

Use translation to quickly and easily separate yourself from The Parasite. Think of it as another weapon in your attack against this enemy. While The Parasite may seem a formidable opponent, it's no match for the self-discovered.

Fourth, The Parasite, Again and Again and Again

In addition to using obvious "I," "you," and "we" statements, The Parasite cleverly tweaks all your emotions in its attempts to persuade you to drink. Here, heightened perception alerts you to The Parasite's con game. It may scream: "This sobriety thing never lasts. You know you're going to give in sooner or later. Drink!" It may be seductive: "Trust me. This time it will be different. You don't have to get drunk. Just one. Do it. Things will be okay, honest. Drink!" It will make you envious: "So, Mary Ann got the promotion. You know that job was meant for you. You deserve to feel better. Drink!" The Parasite tries to belittle you: "I see Joey from the old neighborhood is going to medical school. Oh well, stocking shelves ain't that bad. Yeah, right. Drink!" The Parasite knows what buttons to push. *Resentment:* "Fired!? Who are they to say you drink too much? They all drink. Have a few and you'll show them. You'll get a better job. Drink!" *Anger:* "Damn it! She found your stash. How dare she snoop around like that! Drink!"

The Parasite has no conscience. (That's where you come in.) It exploits your vulnerabilities and viciously attacks your strengths. It wants control in good times and bad.

If you inherit a large sum of money, your Parasite will be ready to celebrate, cheering, "You're rich! It's just like hitting the lottery. Champagne. You deserve it. Can't have a celebration without champagne. Drink!" The Parasite is equally ready to commiserate over any misfortune: "You burnt dinner and the neighbors are due any minute. Drink!" The Parasite turns hard luck into opportunity: "Your flight is delayed three hours. Let's head to the bar. Drink!" Leisure time is fertile ground, and The Parasite wants very much to unwind with you: "Ah! Sunday afternoon all to myself. Drink!" It also wants to share in your sex life: "You can't enjoy a night of passion without some booze. Drink!" The Parasite has the solution for everything, and it's always the same: one more drink. It simply doesn't want to leave you alone (for now).

The Parasite is a short-term pleasure seeker oblivious to consequences. Instant gratification is its goal, as your goals fall by the wayside. The Parasite manipulates all facets of your life under the guise of freedom and frolic. And it is serious about the vow, "Till death do us part."

Your Parasite misses few opportunities. Remember, its only objective is to persuade you, any way it can, to ingest a mood-altering substance and engage in addictive behavior. It wants you to practice alcoholism and addiction. Recognize your self-defeating self-talk and identify it as The Parasite: a detractor to your happiness and sobriety. As the saying goes, "When you least expect it, expect it." And when you do expect it, you'll be ready for it. Your nemesis isn't alcohol, other drugs, gambling, food, or sex. Focus on The Parasite. *It* is your nemesis.

NOTE: The RGM has a version of The Parasite. They use circus metaphors and call it the bear, the tiger, the clown, the alcohol salesman, or the monster. None of these expressions describes the pernicious nature of addiction self-talk as does The Parasite. Also please note that the RGM views its bears, tigers and clowns as "the disease talking." In this RGM formulation, you are powerless and "the disease" is powerful. It's also "cunning" and "baffling" and can only be managed, one day at a time, by joining Bill Wilson's spiritual sobriety circus. You can lay this inane notion to rest. In fact, you must if you're ever to be free of addictions.

Another expression used in the addiction field is "beast." Coined by Rational Recovery founder Jack Trimpey, "beast" is Trimpey's term for what he calls the "addictive voice." In Rational Recovery, the "beast" of addiction is overcome by using Trimpey's process called Addictive Voice Recognition Technique, AVRT™. While Trimpey presents his "beast" as a real entity, overshadowing "the real you," The Parasite, as you now know, is simply a metaphor for the destructive self-talk that we tell ourselves, which leads to addictive behavior. Nevertheless, Rational Recovery offers a fine alternative to traditional 12-step programs. You can learn about Rational Recovery in Trimpey's book, *Rational Recovery: The New Cure for Substance Addiction.*

Cunning, Baffling, Powerful? No Way!

These terms sound grim, don't they? No wonder the RGM insists on calling alcoholism/addiction a disease. The Parasite, too, sounds cunning, baffling, and, dare I say, powerful. While it is persistent, even clever at times, in no way is The Parasite cunning, baffling, or powerful. It is merely the powerless self-talk of addiction. And you don't need to fritter your life away at meetings to overcome it. Your discovery of the dual-mind cycle of addiction alone takes the wind out of The Parasite's sails. Remember, quitting booze/drugs for keeps is a skill you will master—probably fairly easily—now that you're discovering the truth of what you're up against.

In the next chapter, I present the system you will use to remain alcohol and drug free for the rest of your life. This system synthesizes all your discoveries into a clear-cut method for conquering The Parasite. It's not a religious ideology or a professional program reserved for "addiction specialists" who would gladly charge you for their "expertise." Rather, it is the profoundly effective route taken by legions of people who are now enjoying everything that addiction-

and recovery-free living has to offer. Yes, you will quit drinking and drugging without, or in spite of, addiction treatment and recovery groups.

Turn the page and discover the quit-for-good techniques of the self-discovered.

Chapter 11

P.A.W.N.

"There is never a better measure of what a person is than what he does when he's absolutely free to choose."
—William M. Bulger

You are free to practice alcoholism (addiction), or end it. The choice is yours. Science provides valuable information regarding our addictive behavior, survival, and pleasure drives. But it has little to say about ending the bad choices we make (drinking, gambling, drugging, overeating) when pursuing our natural desire for pleasure. Bill Wilson knew that science had not provided effective means to combat the "baffling mind problem" of addiction.

Called the "religious solution" in its early days, AA became the ersatz "scientific" treatment of the time. Over the last several decades, controlled studies have almost universally concluded that AA and the various components of 12-step treatment are at best ineffective, and that at least some of the standard components of such treatment may in fact be harmful; as well, ineffective 12-step treatment (at rehabs) is one of the two most expensive forms of treatment (tied with equally ineffective individual psychotherapy). Even today, those low-cost cognitive-behavioral treatments with the best evidence of efficacy (in terms of reduced drinking) are not noticeably effective in producing long-term abstinence outcomes.

But what if you want to quit? For good! It's a do-it-yourself proposition. Really. Just look.

P.A.W.N. Parasite Awareness Warning & Neutralization

P.A.W.N. wasn't invented. I discovered it and gave it a name, just as I named The Parasite (metaphorically, a mind-parasite) to represent your self-defeating, addiction-feeding self-talk. P.A.W.N. is the very human, concise method used by millions who've knocked off addictive behaviors long before and since AA, the RGM, and the ATI muddied the waters by falsely claiming that everyone is helpless, diseased, and in need of Guru Wilson's "program," the "recovering" community, and professional 12-step addiction treatment.

P.A.W.N. is heightened perception in action. It is not counseling, therapy, or part of any program, religious or otherwise. It's the essence of how legions of people have quit their addictions for good. And as noted in Chapter 1, the 80% of people who quit booze on their own, and the 71% of drug addicts who stop without treatment, are self-discovered, recovery-free, living proof that it works.

Discovering P.A.W.N. is like learning to ride a bicycle. You're a bit wobbly and fall down at first, but mastering the technique is well within your ability. And, like bike riding, this life-long automatic skill will always be there when you need it. Best of all, once you learn it, it's over! There's no need for daily practice, just as there's no need for tentative, one-day-at-a-time sobriety. But as with most worthwhile things, P.A.W.N. takes practice; and with practice, you will defeat The Parasite.

Stop, Listen, Think

Like a vampire, The Parasite runs and hides when exposed to the daylight of P.A.W.N. That's right. As with Thomas Magnum's "little voice," you have the ability to stop, listen and think. Have you made up your (rational) mind to quit booze and other drugs for good? Really made up your mind? If not, stop and listen—use your heightened perception. Do you hear it? Is The Parasite up to its old tricks, suggesting, "For good? That means forever and there ain't no way you're gonna make a commitment like that. Twelve-step programs have it right. Don't quit, just put it off one day at a time. Yeah. I can live with that."

Think! The Parasite loves AA's commitment to never quitting for good. It loves the idea that every day is the day that you might listen to it and act on its behalf. This is a primary reason why you're kept in perpetual "recovery" and told to "keep coming back." The Big Book tells AA wives: "God has either removed your husband's liquor problem or He has not." Gee, when He does remove it, why can't He make it longer than one day at a time?

AA "law" states: Addictions are forever and can only be managed on a daily basis. With P.A.W.N., you will break that "law"! Living in the moment, a day at a time is one thing, but it's a precarious way to stay off booze and other drugs. Why bother, when you can quit any addiction for good? Don't live the disempowering lifestyle that forever labels you as hopelessly "diseased," yet, paradoxically, as also permanently "recovering." Let's get to work and conquer The Parasite.

Start with a Commitment

You are now aware of The Parasite's origin, motives, tactics, and messages (your self-defeating self-talk). This means it's time to fine tune your heightened perception beginning with a Commitment. A Commitment to never drink alcohol or abuse other drugs again. I repeat, a Commitment you make to yourself to never drink alcohol or abuse other drugs again. Not one day at a time, one week, month or year. Never. Say the words aloud now and hear them in your own voice. Say, "I will never drink alcohol or abuse drugs again." Say it again, "I will never drink alcohol or abuse drugs again." Why such an emphasis on this "impossible" Commitment? Because any objection to this Commitment is The Parasite telling you, "You can't say never!" Hear its objections, identify them, spurn them. Say it again, "I will never drink alcohol or abuse drugs again." Now listen. Do you feel The Parasite squirming? Can you "hear" the self-talk now? Is it saying something like, "Never! I can't say *never*. It doesn't feel right. I can't predict the future. I'm not comfortable with saying never."[1]

Picture yourself without a drink ever again. Picture yourself at a party, ball game, the beach, at home, on an airplane, at a restaurant, before, during and after work or school. See yourself, minus booze, forever. How are you feeling? Anxious? Do you feel uncomfortable declaring "I'll never drink again"? Here's the heightened perception: The Parasite is causing your discomfort and anxiety. It doesn't want you saying "never," and during the early days of sobriety it lets you know it. The Parasite, fearing for its life, is concerned that you'll never drink again!

You're now successfully confronting the (former) "baffling problem, which centers in your mind." As we continue, you'll discover how P.A.W.N. combines your heightened perception, your discovery

---

1. Your Commitment refers to never abusing drugs. Prescribed medications [drugs] are invaluable for many people. The next chapter addresses the use of these medicines.

of the dual-mind cycle of addiction, translation, and your Commitment. (Don't sweat the Commitment now. The important thing is to tell it "never" and to "hear" The Parasite's objections.)

P.A.W.N. Awareness

You are already aware of The Parasite. I've stressed using translation to separate from it. Now you will become acutely aware of it. As mentioned above, sobriety's early days bring temporary discomfort. Expect some moodiness, anxiety, and doubts. After all, you've kept The Parasite quite content for a long time. It wants you feeling moody, anxious, and doubtful in the hopes you'll go running for the booze. Here's a tip: Identify your discomfort as a frenzied maneuver performed by a very threatened, survival-driven enemy. Recall the dual-mind cycle of addiction. Your rational brain isn't saying, "Okay, I'll have a few" like it used to. You've thrown a monkey wrench into the works. But the enemy, The Parasite, wants to survive and feels like it's facing the firing squad. It's in a panic because it knows you have the power to quit for good and the Commitment is the nail in its coffin. Identify your discomfort as your Parasite's discomfort, what we might call "Parasite Panic." Remember, The Parasite's only mission is to keep addictions alive. Don't let The Parasite intimidate you. Once it gets the message that you've quit for good your discomfort, the Parasite Panic, will fade.

Here's a Parasite-awareness experiment: Repeat your Commitment aloud now, say, "I will never drink alcohol again. Never." Now listen. You're still probably hearing some of the same old objections: "I can't say never." "I can't predict the future." Now try this: Make this statement aloud: "Just for today, I won't drink." Listen again. Are you hearing acceptance? Something like, "Okay, just for today isn't so bad." Perhaps you heard nothing. If so, remember the old adage, "silence means acceptance."

This exercise shows that The Parasite is content with the idea that you'll drink in the future. It's pacified by "Just for today." But when tomorrow comes, The Parasite is waiting. Day after day after day. It's no wonder the recovery group movement keeps you attending meetings forever. With this non-perceptive thinking (lowered perception) the merry-go-round never stops. If you want off the merry-go-round, don't pacify The Parasite, and when The Parasite panics, you'll be ready and aware.

Social functions, meeting new people, facing a crisis, or the joy of good fortune can all produce feelings of anxiety, apprehension, or elation. But a panicky Parasite will do what it does best: trying to persuade you to act on your emotions through addictive behavior. Since The Parasite is a hedonistic, short-term pleasure seeker, it may propose: "A few drinks will relax you. Have a couple before the job interview." The Parasite doesn't care when you vomit on the shoes of what could have been your future employer. So, be aware.

Unless you act on The Parasite's behalf, it's powerless. Think of The Parasite as a lowly pest, a nuisance that in reasonably short order will stop its incessant badgering once it understands that you never drink or abuse other drugs. The awareness in P.A.W.N. exposes The Parasite in all its naked infamy. And The Parasite hates being exposed that way.

The P.A.W.N Warning

"Keep it green" (your memory of drunken yesterdays) and "Remember your last drunk" are AA slogans. Through drunkalogs, which are personal stories of drunkenness and ensuing 12-step salvation, these slogans help the penitent recall his intoxicated hell on earth. At some spiritual level, dredging up past pain is supposed to serve as a warning, which will relieve your compulsion to drink. This approach is a joke. The Parasite remembers all drunken yesterdays fondly. It filters out the pain and highlights the pleasure (of feeling high): "Okay, so you got everyone upset when you showed up drunk, just make sure you eat something next time." Old hurts and guilt may lead to short-term sobriety, but they only serve to keep you in long-term "recovery." Don't bank that recalling your drunken past will keep you from imbibing. Let your awareness of The Parasite serve as your alarm because The Parasite is always up to no good.

The P.A.W.N. warning means *beware!* In the old TV show, "Lost In Space," The Space Family Robinson had a handy B-9 robot (no self-respecting space family would be without one) that was intuitively aware of impending peril. With a computerized bellow, the robot would shout, "Warning, warning, warning" and "Danger, danger, danger." You too are now keenly aware of The Parasite, and that awareness translates into "warning" and "danger." Whenever you detect Parasite activity, be forewarned—it never shows up to pay a friendly visit.

Neutralize The Parasite

Following P.A.W.N. to its conclusion means telling The Parasite to get lost. This is the essence of P.A.W.N., and the self-discovered are recovery-free, living proof that it works. Let's get going and master the skill of neutralizing The Parasite. Like the day you mastered bike riding, you'll be two-wheelin' in no time.

One of the standard AA one-day-at-a-time ways of avoiding drinking is diversions—doing something, anything, else when the urge to drink becomes strong. The self-discovered aren't concerned with having a toolbox full of diversions. Should The Parasite come calling, you won't be able to take a mind-clearing walk if you're on an airplane or driving to work (in fact, you may drive straight to the liquor store). Similarly, taking a shower or engaging in a hobby aren't feasible when you're out to dinner or on the job. By all means, though, if diversions prove helpful, and it's possible to engage in them, fine. But what happens when you can't? Here, people in recovery are particularly vulnerable. They need diversions. The self-discovered don't. Without a meeting, a sponsor to phone, or some group member coming to the rescue, their AA training kicks into overdrive. Their baffling brain problem says: "You're powerless and can't trust your own judgments. People understand when you relapse. They may not like it, but hey, you've got the disease." (This is pure Parasite in action.) Unless AA's Higher Powers intervene, relapse, repentance, and contemplation is a guarantee.

I've said that I can't teach you motivation. No one can. What I've given you is the "secret" of the self-discovered: the knowledge that you can quit any addiction for good and live "recovery" free. "Neutralizing" The Parasite is done with attitude, not dependency groups, sponsors, programs, or higher powers. Look at some of your discoveries:

1) The Dual Mind Cycle of Addiction explains addictive thinking and behavior.

2) Heightened Perception gives you the power to stop, listen, and think before you act on addictive desires.

3) Translation of addictive self-talk instantly separates you from The Parasite.

4) Urges (following physical withdrawal) come from a panicky Parasite up to its old survival tricks.

5) Urges/cravings pass, and become progressively less intense as time goes by.

6) The Parasite is powerless. It needs you to act on its behalf.

You understand The Parasite now. You've discovered its origin, motives, tactics, and addictive self-talk. Alcoholism/addiction is no longer AA's "cunning, baffling, powerful" disease. Remember that Commitment you made? (If you didn't, or couldn't, don't worry. It takes a few punches to KO The Parasite.) Let it be your rudder. Forcefully remind yourself that Parasite-driven behaviors are not acceptable and that booze and drugs (or whatever compulsive behavior caused you harm) are something you have quit and something that you never do. (It still feels uncomfortable to say that, doesn't it?) No matter how miserable you may feel, know that it's temporary, non-life-threatening Parasite panic. Remember, using P.A.W.N. takes some work; then again, weren't a few bruised knees and elbows worth learning to ride a bike? Utilize your heightened perception, make use of translation, review the dual-mind cycle and stay focused on your Commitment. Neutralizing The Parasite, telling it to get lost, becomes second nature in reasonably short order (a few weeks for most people).

Waking up each day thinking, "I'm in recovery, what must I do to keep sober today?" is the last thing you need. Be it New Year's Eve, Saturday night, or Monday night football it doesn't matter—you have quit and you never drink or abuse other drugs. You're not working a one-day-at-a-time recovery program. You're living a recovery-free lifetime of *discovery*.

Being Human

Human fallibility is not an excuse for addictive behavior. It is an element of it. Our freedom of choice is what makes us human. Should you renege on your Commitment, know that as a free-willed, thinking human being, you made the choice. You are personally and morally responsible for your behavior. Immediately renew your Commitment, learn from your experience, address your ambivalence, and get on with discovery. Feeling guilty only weighs you down and provides fuel for The Parasite. Also, know that the mistake of having a drink does not have to lead to a drunk, as you were wrongly told in AA.

But understand, the more you decide to drink, the stronger The Parasite grows. And as you get drunker, The Parasite screams for more. While The Parasite may trip you up a time or two, forcefully remind yourself that "relapse, repent and contemplate" is recovering behavior that you've left behind and no longer accept.

Drinking after a period of sobriety quickly recharges The Parasite's batteries to reassert itself and to once again take over. And with The Parasite in the driver's seat, you were on autopilot—drinking, drugging, gambling, and eating like there was no tomorrow. Use P.A.W.N. Neutralize The Parasite, and take pride in your Commitment.

Abstinence Violation Effect

In their 1985 landmark book, *Relapse Prevention*, Doctors G. Alan Marlatt and Judith R. Gordon introduce the Abstinence Violation Effect (AVE). AVE is a measure of how badly one might feel if abstinence is broken. But merry-go-round operators pervert Marlatt and Gordon's research. They use it to "prove" how powerless you are and how badly you should feel after taking a drink/drug. Sure, you'll be disappointed, but 12-step operators exploit your disappointment. Here's how: The intensity of AVE is proportionate to two factors: a) the length of sobriety achieved; and b) the degree of commitment to abstinence. (Better yet, think of yourself as refraining from booze and other drugs. "Abstinence" rings of RGM puritanism.) "Even the researchers know you're powerless," operators say, "that's why they formulated AVE."

There's a vast difference between relapsing due to the being a victim of the supposed progressive, incurable disease of the RGM, and choosing to resume your addictive behavior. "Addictive disease" implies powerlessness, "baffling brain problems," and the need for treatment and recovery. "Choosing" explains this as a reversible human behavior, which you consciously acted out at your emotional mind's behest. Put this choice in proper perspective: against your better judgment, you obeyed The Parasite and made a rash decision. Just as a scoop of ice cream doesn't wipe out the positives from months of dieting, the mistake of having a drink doesn't blow your ability to get back on your booze- and drug-free diet. Don't beat yourself up—focus on punching out The Parasite.

Don't Count Time, Count on Self-Worth

Throw out the sobriety time clock. Your self-worth is not determined by AA's standard of "sober" time. You're not involved in one-upmanship with anyone based on length of sobriety. This isn't a contest; it's your life. Counting "clean time" is a way for others to measure how "good" you've been. It's for those who collect sobriety chips. It elevates their recovering status, allows them to lord it over those with less "time," and boosts their delicate self-esteem. But a relapse plummets them back to square one. They then sink even lower when they must turn in their chips, reset their sobriety clocks back to zero, and perform another 90 in 90. (At least, this happens with those who are honest about relapsing.)

Don't buy into their guilt trip, or that you need to set a new "dry date." Take pride in whatever sobriety you had and keep building on it. Whether you have ten years or ten days is irrelevant because you are always a worthwhile individual, and because your goal is to be happy and healthy—not to "win" in some inane competition. Playing AA's "I have more sobriety than you" time-counting game is for the recovering, not the discovering.

Avoiding the Abstinence Violation Effect is as simple as living your Commitment and never drinking or abusing other drugs again. Does this still sound impossible? Here we go again: any thought of the impossibility of not drinking or drugging, any feeling of doubt, is classic Parasite panic. Treatment-savvy merry-go-round operators insist that you need counseling, relapse prevention programs and meetings for life. You need none of it. All you need to do is stay focused on the Commitment and practice the principles of P.A.W.N.

Here's a tip: Since you cannot prove, to anyone else's satisfaction, that you have quit booze and other drugs for good, (because the RGM has been very successful in spreading the falsehood that addiction is an incurable, progressive disease, characterized by spontaneous relapse), don't even try. (Do we ask former cigarette smokers to prove that they have quit?) Let your actions speak for themselves.

You don't have to prove anything to anyone. Your Commitment is all that matters.

Choose Wisely

RGM members will do and say almost anything to undermine your confidence and your Commitment. They insist that your declaration to never drink again is a delusion from a diseased mind. They threaten you with the bleak predictions of jails, institutions, or death unless you shape up, drop the denial, and get with The Program. Not surprisingly, the "I can't commit to quitting for good, so you can't commit" mentality permeates the RGM's brain-baffled recovering souls. If they have to work The Program, you have to work it, too. They scorn anything different as the "easier, softer way." Ignore their nonsense.

Because of their self-professed powerlessness and character defects, 12-step members can't take personal responsibility for mastering their addictive behavior. Only Higher Powers can provide that miracle. But even in their one-day-at-a-time sobriety, The Parasite is in charge. It has them forever recovering (but never recovered) and fearful of relapse. It has them running to meetings and counselors, praying to gods of their own imaginations, and signing up others to join their club. The Parasite loves AA and the RGM. It loves impressionable newcomers and their indoctrination into a society that teaches them that addictions are forever. The Parasite loves AVE. and the fact that relapse, thanks to Bill Wilson and the RGM, is a daily prospect for everyone "in recovery."

Engaging in abusive addictive behaviors is a choice, an unfortunate destructive choice, but a choice nonetheless. The bottom line is that quitting and staying quit are choices also. This is nothing akin to the failed "Just say no" campaign of the Reagan Administration. The Parasite loves "Just say no." To The Parasite, "No" means, "Not now, but feel free to pester me later." "No" just doesn't punch out The Parasite like "never" does.

More Fun with Brussel Sprouts

Here's another experiment: Picture yourself at the places where you've engaged in addictive behaviors. Go all out. Open up your senses and hear the sounds, smell the scents, and taste the tastes as well. Where are you? At a party? The bar or club? A Friday night card game or sporting event? Maybe you're in a park, on a street corner, or in the basement or bedroom. In your mind's eye, see and sense yourself in these situations. Take your time. Got it? Now, firmly state: "I will never eat brussel sprouts again." Say it now, "I will never eat brussel sprouts again." Listen. Do you hear it? Unless you have addicted yourself to brussel sprouts, I doubt you heard much of anything. Maybe a subtle, "Yeah, so what?" but certainly no Parasite. How would you feel if you had truly committed to never eating brussel sprouts? Would it seem impossible? Could you be reasonably confident in your ability to never eat them again? A Commitment to never drink or drug only seems impossible because The Parasite doesn't want you saying "never" to its life force: booze and drugs. It couldn't care less about brussel sprouts.

Airplanes, Sharks, and Monkeys

Think of it this way: could you be reasonably sure that you'd keep your commitment if you vowed to never sky dive, swim with sharks, or eat monkey brains? Odds on, the answer is "yes." Still, being the noncommittal, fallible human being you are, you have reservations. What if airplane trouble forces you to parachute to safety? What if you land in shark-infested waters and must swim to an island inhabited by natives who eat monkey brains? What if your survival meant eating monkey brains, too? "Never say never" is our national motto, especially when it comes to addictions. And since you only postpone your boozing in AA, you will never quit. You will however, be expected to dutifully join the 12-step church-basement society to put off one-day-at-a-time doing something you're capable of right now. State your Commitment, use P.A.W.N., and quit!

What If?

Of course, the above scenario is outlandish. And since you haven't addicted yourself to sky diving, swimming with sharks, or monkey brains, refraining from them isn't a big deal to you or The Parasite. The point is that The Parasite can be just as outlandish.

Here's how: What if you make the Commitment and find yourself in the Sahara with only beer to drink? What if you "had" to drink because no one brought anything but booze on the camping trip? What if world hunger would end if only you drank with philanthropic space aliens? What if . . . what if . . . what if . . . Where the Commitment is concerned, all "what ifs" come directly from The Parasite.

Most "what ifs" are simply reservations that won't stop you from making a commitment. But with addictions, The Parasite has a trunk full of "what ifs." It tries anything to keep you from saying "never." That way, it can plague you and the entire recovering community at every meeting, every day, one day at a time for the rest of your lives.

A Different Drummer

So there you have it, the essence of the self-discovered: P.A.W.N., your all-in-one tool for staying booze, drug and recovery free.

Henry David Thoreau wrote:

If a man does not keep pace with his companions, perhaps it is because he hears a different drummer. Let him step to the music he hears, however measured or far away.

RGM members despise those who march to a "different drummer." Seeing such people forces them to look at their own condition, and quite often they don't like what they see: accepting themselves as diseased for life, with only Bill Wilson's spiritual teachings to offer one-day-at-a-time respite.

To the RGM, "different drummers" means that their recovery monopoly is jeopardized. But are monopolies a good thing? As a kid, did you ever want to do something because "everybody's doing it?" And were you knocked down a peg with that parental pearl, "If everyone's jumping off a bridge, are you going to jump off too?" You're no longer a kid. Just because the RGM wants you "in recovery," are you going to "jump off the bridge" with them? That doesn't make sense when your health, happiness, and sobriety are at stake. Stepping to the music of discovery and P.A.W.N. is like hearing Thoreau's different drummer, only the beat isn't so measured or far away. It's for real and it's here, right now. Embrace the music. Do what's right for you to beat your addiction. That's what matters. Take P.A.W.N. and use it.

P.A.W.N. Pocket Summary

Parasite: "Gotta have it." "I want it." "I need it." "You can have a couple."

Awareness: Heightened Perception.Dual Mind Cycle of Addiction.

Translation: "The Parasite's gotta have it." "The Parasite wants it." "The Parasite needs it." "The Parasite wants to have a couple." Parasite Panic.

Warning: Danger. The Parasite's up to no good.

Neutralize: Attitude! Nuke it! Get lost! The Commitment.

Chapter 12

The Myth of Relapse Triggers

"The devil made me do it the first time; the second
time I done it on my own."
—Willy Nelson

H.A.L.T.

H.A.L.T. is yet another RGM contrivance designed to keep you powerless. It stands for Hungry, Angry, Lonely, or Tired, all of which are supposedly high-risk conditions that lead to relapse. Meredith Gould is an AA recruiter who penned the Hazelden publication, *Staying Sober: Tips for Working a Twelve Step Program of Recovery.* What's frightening is that Gould is a sociologist who incorporates her 12-step dogma into her practice. Please read her take on H.A.L.T.:

> You can do yourself a huge favor by using H.A.L.T., a handy mnemonic device to trace your unwanted addictive feelings to being either Hungry, Angry, Lonely, or Tired. There are few, if any, addicts on the face of the earth whose addiction isn't massively triggered by one of these factors. You're headed for even deeper trouble if all apply and aren't quickly addressed.

Gould's misleading statement glorifies powerlessness. She promotes the idea that almost anything, anytime, can "massively trigger" another addictive episode. Just being awake puts you in relapse jeopardy. Are you ever Hungry, Angry, Lonely or Tired? If you believe Gould and the rest of the 12-step "experts," it's hardly surprising that under the self-imposed pressure of a H.A.L.T. moment you would you fall back into addictive behavior. And if you get into deep trouble by becoming Hungry, Angry, Lonely, and Tired all at the same time, and your booze-provoking H.A.L.T. symptoms aren't dealt with, it's back to John Barleycorn for you—because Gould and her RGM cronies make sobriety contingent upon maintaining creature comfort at all times, something which is clearly impossible.

Gould's "massively triggered" assertion is most disturbing, though it's the party line in 12-step circles. As a good merry-go-round operator, Gould offers you the usual remedies: attending AA meetings; working the steps; exercising; getting proper rest; letting go of anger; taking hot baths; and eating when hungry. While diet, exercise and proper rest are good, they are not the key to freedom from addiction any more than submission to AA's Higher Power is the key. Gould's remedies reflect the tentative sobriety mindset of all "recovering" people—you can never quit any addiction for good. Even under the best circumstances, the most you can hope for is a 24-hour reprieve, and even that's in jeopardy if you become Hungry, Angry, Lonely or Tired.

Gould and her colleagues haven't the slightest clue of how to permanently quit any addiction. Infected with Parasite panic, these professional 12-step operators pass it on to their clients: "H.A.L.T. symptoms are very powerful and can lead you back to drinking in an instant. The way to combat H.A.L.T. is by following our tips for working a 12-step program." Finding excuses for never making the Commitment to quit is their true expertise. Outside forces such as H.A.L.T. must be responsible for their addictive behavior (because they've abdicated their power to choose), so they assign ordinary events the power to derail their precarious recoveries.

As one of the newly self-discovered, you have put a stop to this H.A.L.T. nonsense. You now know that resuming addictive behavior is done by *choice*, by listening to The Parasite; it doesn't happen because of the "massive trigger[s]" from everyday occurrences. There are no relapse monsters lurking around every corner.

It Must Be Something You Ate

Can your diet cause alcohol-drinking urges? That depends on your definition. If urges mean, "Can what you eat or don't eat cause you to drink alcohol?", the answer is "no." If it means, "Can what you eat or don't eat cause physical/emotional discomfort that can be relieved by using alcohol?", then the answer is "yes," whether or not you were ever addicted.

Nutritional factors are largely ignored in the addiction field. There are clinicians and addiction researchers however, who would like to change that. Indeed, they say that without the proper diet, both your physical and mental health will suffer. This sounds reasonable. They also say that improper diets initiate cravings that put alcoholics at high risk for relapse. This also sounds reasonable—to people "in recovery." But it's unreasonable for the self-discovered. I'll explain: In their book, *Under The Influence*, clinical psychologist James R. Milam and co-author Katherine Ketcham cite three essentials for overcoming the "disease of alcoholism":

1. Understanding the nature of the disease; 2. Nutritional discipline; 3. AA participation.

They spell out the second of these factors in detail:

> The alcoholic must receive vitamin and mineral supplements in order to repair the cellular damage caused by years of drinking If, after treatment, the alcoholic maintains a life-long dietary regime with appropriate vitamin and mineral supplements, his addiction will remain dormant and he will not be threatened by the craving for alcohol that plagues so many alcoholics for months and years after their last drink.

This statement is false. While vitamin and mineral supplements are routinely used during medically supervised detox, and cellular repair is fostered by their use, to assert that without them the alcoholic is in peril of relapse is just that—an unproven assertion. While we all benefit from good nutrition, there is no real evidence that it is necessary for combating alcoholic cravings. In other words, daily Big Macs don't create "months and years" of alcohol craving, nor will addictions "remain dormant" if you eat tofu and bean sprouts.

I'm not attempting to denigrate the health benefits of eating right. A healthy diet can significantly increase your quality of life. Considering the damage caused by years of substance abuse, a good diet and the use of at least some supplements makes sense. Avoiding refined sugars and caffeine, for example, reduces irritability and allows you to sleep better. But to suggest "bad" diets will throw you into sobriety-busting craving frenzies is addiction treatment industry voodoo. Remember, Milam and Ketchum work from the lowered perception of merry-go-round operators. They view alcoholism as an incurable, progressive disease. They need reasons to explain the failed treatment practices and the relapse-repent-contemplate cycle of the ATI/RGM. The failure of "recovering" alcoholics and addicts to follow their prescribed "lifelong dietary regime" provides the treatment industry with yet another alibi with which to excuse its failure.

There is no harm in following a diet as outlined in Milam and Ketcham's book. In fact, it's almost certainly good for you. They offer an effective, high-protein, low-carbohydrate diet to help control the alcoholic's chronic low blood sugar level (hypoglycemia). So follow their diet, if you choose. But bear in mind that diet plans are not required to permanently quit booze or any other drug. (PS: Exercise isn't necessary either, but even mild exercise will lead to a healthier and probably happier you. A comprehensive medical check-up is a good idea, too.)

More Triggers—Walking Down Memory Lane

But relapse triggers do exist. The sights, sounds, tastes and smells of addiction ring Pavlovian bells. Even grandma's holiday eggnog can reawaken the craving for self-indulgent pleasures and spark the dual-mind cycle. These stimuli include: a favorite mug, shot or drinking glass; any type of pill; cold cash or a paycheck; dollar bills and straws; ice cubes clinking in a glass; mirrors; hypodermic needles; driving past a bar or liquor store; prescription bottles; razor blades; seeing an old drinking buddy; and songs associated with drinking or using.

Relapse triggers are nothing more than The Parasite recalling the pleasurable effects of booze and other drugs: "That bar sure looks inviting, I'd love to stop in for a couple," or "I wish this prescription bottle was filled with Percocet." Immediately use translation: "That bar sure looks uninviting, and The Parasite would love to stop in for a couple"; "The Parasite wishes this prescription bottle was filled with Percocet."

Relapse triggers have no power. Recognize the self-talk that goads you to drink or use when you see, hear, taste, or smell something related to your addicted past. It's only The Parasite walking down memory lane. Incidentally, these Parasite memories fade in frequency and intensity with every sober day.

Unless you opt for the cloistered life, you cannot avoid all these "triggers," nor do you need to. You can even enjoy non-alcoholic beer and wine without being "triggered" to move on to the real thing. But using these beverages is a personal call. Some contain .5% alcohol, and you need to do what you're at ease with and works for you.

(NOTE: It's virtually impossible to get drunk on .5% near beer. American beer normally contains between 4% and 5% alcohol.

Budweiser, for example, contains 5% alcohol, and Bud Light 4.2%. So, you'd have to drink ten .5% near beers to equal the alcohol content of a single bottle of Bud or eight-and-a-half near beers to equal the alcohol content of a single Bud Light.)

But what about prescription medication? Debate rages in RGM circles concerning whether to take or not to take prescribed meds. Rehab "treatment" however, often has patients informing their doctors that as "recovering alcoholics/addicts," they should never be prescribed any mind-altering drugs. This debasing self-disclosure stems from "addictive disease" thinking, in which it's believed that taking a mind-altering medicine will "trigger" the alcoholic/addict's "incurable progressive disease." Of course, there is no empirical evidence to support this belief, and when used as prescribed, prescription medications should not pose a problem for you. Still, this too is a personal call and you must do what is right for you.

Ask yourself: Do I need narcotic pain relievers, or can Advil handle my root canal? Do I need a sleep aid, or will a change in diet (no caffeine after 3:00 pm for instance) help me to get my z's? Should I suffer after my surgery, or should I take a morphine shot to relieve my pain and help me to recuperate? Only you can answer these questions. Again, taking prescription medicines will not trigger any addictive disease, and when used as prescribed, they should not cause you any problems.

I don't pretend to know your pain threshold, your sleeping pattern, nor can I monitor your diet. But remember, you're self-discovered now. You've heightened your perception, you know the dual-mind cycle of addiction, you're aware of The Parasite, you know how to use translation, you've made your Commitment, and you have P.A.W.N. There's no need to fear these medicines. They cannot be abused unless you *choose* to abuse them. And with your newfound freedom from addiction and recovery, why in hell would you choose to do that?

Unlike Pavlov's dogs, you have the ability to reason. While you may unwisely choose to drink or abuse drugs, nothing can trigger you to do so. When you keep in mind that triggers simply set off the dual-mind cycle, you can use P.A.W.N., neutralize The Parasite and go about your recovery-free business.

Warning Signs: More Excuses

Relapse prevention programs focus on all the reasons that make recovery a day-to-day crapshoot. Since you're not expected to quit for good, the RGM and ATI have devised warning signs of relapse. These are yet more excuses to justify the behavior of people who choose to booze it up: denial; compulsive behavior; defensiveness; discontinuing addiction treatment; dissatisfaction with life; frustration; anger; anxiety; tension; idle daydreaming/wishful thinking; imposing sobriety on others; impulsive behavior; irregular AA attendance; irregular eating habits; irregular sleeping habits; irritation with friends/family; keeping secrets; listlessness; loss of control; loss of daily structure; loss of self-confidence; lying; minor depression; open rejection of AA; periods of confusion; resentments; self-pity; and thoughts of social drinking (which you know are The Parasite's thoughts).

This list comes from the now-defunct Fair Oaks Hospital in New Jersey. Once known as the Betty Ford Clinic of the East, Fair Oaks has closed its doors because of financial scandal. The former rehab's parent company, NME Psychiatric Hospitals, Inc., has admitted to several counts of conspiracy, illegal remunerations, and insurance fraud. But in the ATI world, you would hear a different tale: NME executives weren't crooks; they were diseased. Big money triggered the execs who didn't recognize the warning signs: wishful thinking, keeping secrets, defensiveness and lies. They were powerless over their money addiction and illegal behavior. If they had only joined Addictions Anonymous or Sinners Anonymous, they could have been recovering from their sickness: greed. If this sounds ridiculous, it is. Warning signs of relapse are just another RGM device to keep you powerless and to justify the RGM's failed treatment policies.

No More Excuses

Look, you know The Parasite is going to bug you for a time; and you know how to neutralize it. Relapse triggers and "warning signs" are part of the Bill babble you no longer speak. By now, I'm sure that you see how the RGM manipulates and capitalizes on all life circumstances to convince you of your powerlessness and that you may relapse at any time. Parasite-controlled "recovering" folk grant absolute power to the people, places, and things that, in their "diseased" minds, will send *them* running for the bottle. So, they want *you* to stay away from anywhere where liquor might be served—weddings, ballgames, and barbeques; even family get-togethers are considered "slippery places." According to the RGM, holidays, anniversaries, indeed almost any event or stress is a perilous, booze-triggering minefield.

It's sad that the Higher Powers of the RGM are so particular about where, when and how they protect the "recovering." But you have the advantage of P.A.W.N. You know the dual-mind cycle of addiction. You make the conscious decision to break your Commitment and drink alcohol; nothing "triggers" you to do so.

The self-discovered have been quitting booze and other drugs for ages. Either by education or nature, we understand the dual-mind cycle and have made our Commitment to never drink. Something, someone, or someplace is not always lurking out there to derail us. The devil may make recovering people drink, but for the self-discovered, The Parasite can only try.

The next chapter addresses the RGM's, "family disease of codependency." It exposes the recovery rituals and beliefs which keep the family and friends of substance abusers spinning on the codependency merry-go-round. As with all the self-discovered, "codependents" will discover how to change their self-defeating behavior now and for good, without meetings, sponsors, or "recovering" for the rest of their lives.

Chapter 13

Beware the Codependency Cartel

"The best way to predict the future is to create it."
—Peter F. Drucker

Living with an addict doesn't conjure up Norman Rockwell images. The recovery group movement is shrewdly aware of the plight families in such situations face, and it gladly comes to their "rescue." In reality, that "rescue" consists of ensnaring the entire family in 12-step recovery groups.

This chapter will resonate with those spinning on the codependency merry-go-round and offers sure-fire ways off it. In fact, the empowering techniques described here apply to everyone seeking a recovery-free life.

Let's say that dad is the drinker in your home. According to RGM dictates, dad, mom, and junior must all become Bill Wilson groupies through AA, Al-Anon, and Alateen, respectively. Case closed. Now everyone can (and must) work his or her recovery program. They'll blissfully "walk the walk and talk the talk" as outlined by their 12-step mentors. The family that "steps" together stays together. Right?

What's Wrong with This Picture?

Are the rosy images of dad, mom, and junior skipping hand in hand into the sunset of 12-step serenity the stuff off dreams? Not if the codependency cartel has anything to say about it. And believe me, they have plenty to say.

The codependency cartel is part of the RGM and is made up of 12-step, AA spin-off sects. These sects are designed to make Bill Wilson disciples out of the family and friends of substance abusers. They also minister to people with non-alcohol related relationship problems. These groups include:

Al-Anon for family and friends of alcoholics
Alateen for adolescents concerned with another's drinking/drugging
ACOA—Adult Children of Alcoholics
CODA—Codependents Anonymous
GamAnon for family and friends concerned with another's gambling

New members, whether in AA or codependency groups, are termed "pigeons." Group elders carefully watch them during the 12-step indoctrination process. They even go so far as to suggest that pigeons break off ties with non-program friends and family, because "normies" (non-members) just don't understand "program people" and can lead the pigeon away from the fellowship, away from The Truth.

But the sad truth is that the codependency cartel, like AA, is anti-family. The fellowship(s) must come first, which deeply divides already troubled homes. This anti-family stance is cleverly explained away by reinforcing the false notion that without their 12-step groups, people "in recovery" (meaning the entire family) will surely perish, ending up jailed, institutionalized, or dead.

The reality is that families touched by addictions do not always survive intact. Separation and divorce are often unavoidable, because by the time addicts seek help, many times their damaged relationships have reached the point of no return. But this isn't always the case; not all relationships involving addicts are so badly damaged. Still, even many salvageable relationships break up as the direct result of RGM meddling, and the misguidance of sponsors and codependency counselors.

Al-Anon sponsors commonly counsel a pigeon that his or her addicted loved one is doomed to failure unless that loved one sticks with AA, even if he or she is securely sober (and, in many cases, has been for years). The brainwashed Al-Anon spouse then demands that the former alcoholic attend AA, and if he or she refuses, it often spells the end of the relationship. Another example is that "recovering" spouses often undergo marked personality changes as they become immersed in the fellowship. Sacred bonds develop as they spend inordinate hours with their "new family," and home life takes a back seat to their "recovering" friends, who "appreciate" them. Worse, "13th stepping" is common in virtually all 12-step groups; sexual relationships form, and "the rooms" of Al-Anon and AA often resemble pick-up joints. Meanwhile, the spouse at home is unaware that much more than spiritual healing is taking place. In fact, at least some of the more conscientious AA members warn newcomers of the sexual advances of 12-step predators. They even have a cautionary slogan: "Work the program from the waist up." But, unfortunately, marriages are destroyed and trusting newcomers are abused before most learn of this slogan or this unlucky #13.

It All Stems from Bill W.

In addition to his 12-steps, Bill Wilson penned the 12 traditions to clarify AA's mission and to ensure its continued growth. The code-pendency cartel operates by the same codes. Alcoholics Anonymous World Services, Inc. has copyright to Wilson's book, *Twelve Steps and Twelve Traditions*. The first tradition explains the importance of AA's welfare over all else, including you and your family:

> Each member of Alcoholics Anonymous is but a small part of a great whole. AA must continue to live or most of us will surely die. Hence our common welfare comes first. But individual welfare follows close afterward.

In truth, individual welfare is a low priority. Read the following, also from *Twelve Steps and Twelve Traditions*. After you read each selection, we'll translate this slice of Bill babble into plain English.

> The AA member has to conform to the principles of recovery. His life actually depends upon obedience to spiritual principles.
> *(Translation: You must become a Bill Wilson groupie. Your life actually depends upon obedience to Wilson's spiritual teachings.)*

> If he deviates too far, the penalty is sure and swift; he sickens and dies.
> *(Translation: Unless you obey and live by AA standards, you will go insane, rot in jail, or die.)*

> Moreover, he finds he cannot keep this priceless gift unless he gives it away. Neither he nor anybody else can survive unless he carries the AA message.
> *(Translation: You must proselytize the AA faith and recruit new members, otherwise we all perish.)*

Most individuals cannot recover unless there is a group. Realization dawns that he is but a small part of a great whole; that no personal sacrifice is too great for preservation of the Fellowship.
(Translation: You are a soldier in Bill Wilson's 12-step army and good soldiers make sacrifices and follow orders.)

He learns that the clamor of desires and ambitions within him must be silenced whenever these could damage the group.
(Translation: All desires and ambitions, i.e. marriage, dating, divorce, having children, job changes, vacations, investments, etc. must be in AA's best interest.)

It becomes plain that the group must survive or the individual will not.
(Translation: Without AA, you are nothing. The fellowship equals life.)

Many people see through this 12-step sham and avoid the codependency cartel and AA. Others are not so perceptive (yet). While family and friends want the best for their addicted loved one, surrendering their common sense to the mystical musings of Bill W. can be the ultimate living nightmare. From the Big Book:

Years of living with an alcoholic is almost sure to make any wife or child neurotic. The entire family is, to some extent, ill.

Nothing will help the man who is off on a spiritual tangent so much as the wife who adopts a sane spiritual program, making a better practical use of it.

A sane spiritual program? Not only do Wilson's 12-step clubs conquer the diseases of alcoholism and codependency, they now triumph over neuroses, and that's not all. Read some of Joe Klaas's unrelenting spiritual/religious exhortations from his recovery book, *The Twelve Steps to Happiness:*

The steps present by far the most successful way for incurable drug addicts to recover. Incurable gamblers overcome their compulsion with the Twelve Steps. Compulsive overeaters who have failed to solve their problem by any known diet plan return to sane eating habits by means of these Steps. They enable nicotine addicts who never before were able to stop smoking to knock off cigarettes forever, one day at a time. They enable compulsive debtors to spend sanely and accumulate wealth. The unconquerable disease of co-dependence is subdued by the Twelve Steps. People diagnosed with terminal cancer, AIDS and other deadly diseases survive with the Steps.

The steps enable the afflicted to survive incurable diseases, not by science or logic, but by miraculous recovery It is a supernatural Power greater than ourselves.

Perhaps if we still think the Twelve Steps, which put only that Higher Power to work on our problems, will not work for AIDS or cancer, we ought to take an inventory of what other aspects of human life we think would be too much for God. God can't handle a virus? Or a malignancy? Come on. What else can God not handle? What other things are more powerful than God?

Say "hallelujah!" The presumption and arrogance of the preceding passage is positively breathtaking. Joe Klaas and his breed talk about recovery, but they are fanatical missionaries whose singular mission is to tout miracle cures and fill the ranks of their 12-step recovery group movement; their goal, in fact, is to convert the entire world.

Meanwhile, you, the "codependent," have been manipulatively diagnosed as being very, very ill. Yet we know that Bill Wilson's "program" does not benefit most people who try it. This includes people suffering from the "unconquerable disease of codependence."

Your "illness," of course, is the brainchild of the RGM. The "disease of alcoholism" has morphed into the "family disease" of codependency. Diseased family members, like good AA members, must drop their denial, admit to their powerlessness and unmanageable lives, and find deliverance through working the steps. Then Al-Anon, CODA, ACOA, and Alateen, like eagle-eyed conductors, will all be there to punch their one-way tickets to "serenity."

Codependency: Another Incurable "Disease"

We all have challenges. And people often rise to meet them with determination, integrity and resilience. While they don't always do it perfectly, or joyously, they do it. An addicted loved one is a challenge, too. And you can meet this challenge without "recovering" for the rest of your life.

But the addiction treatment industry doesn't want you to know this. Indeed, they tell you the exact opposite. A particularly egregious example of the 12-step party line on this issue is found in Anne Wilson Schaef's book, *When Society Becomes an Addict*. Please read the following carefully as Schaef highlights the thoughts of codependen-cy researcher Sharon Wegscheider-Cruse:

> Wegscheider-Cruse defines co-dependence as "an addiction to anoth-er person or persons and their problems, or to a relationship and its problems." She notes some insurance companies are now recognizing that co-dependence is a primary disease that has an onset, a definable course, and a predictable outcome. In other words, co-dependence is not a symptom of something else. . . .
> A co-dependent is a person who is currently involved in a love or marriage relationship with an addict, had at least one alcoholic par-ent or grandparent, and/or grew up in an emotionally repressive fam-ily-co-dependents make up about 96 percent of the population. . . .
> [I]t is not enough to treat the individual who is abusing alcohol, drugs, or whatever it is. Instead, we must treat the individual's whole family system, which is an addictive system. As a result more empha-sis is being placed on treating the co-dependent.

Wegscheider-Cruse and other disease theorists love to state that codependence follows the road map of legitimate diseases: onset, definable course, and predictable outcome pattern. Therefore, co-dependence must also be a legitimate disease. Friends, if we buy into this mumbo jumbo, we're all in for a whole lot of trouble.

What's lost here is that we're talking about human behavior, not disorders caused by disease pathogens or genetic effects. We're also talking about a "proof" so poor that, using the same criteria, attend-ing a baseball game could also be defined as a "disease": (onset) you go to a baseball game; (definable course) the teams play for nine innings; (predictable outcome pattern) one team wins, one loses, and you go home. Thus, attending a baseball game is a legitimate disease. This isn't much more ridiculous than defining "codependency" as a disease.

While people living with addicts face innumerable challenges, they are far from diseased. Amazingly, we have forgotten, or possi-bly never knew, that the word "codependence" was only recently coined by the recovery group movement. And like its sister "dis-ease," alcoholism, codependency cannot be cured. But you can recov-er, one day at a time, when you hitch up with the codependency cartel.

Codependency responds to treatment as well as alcoholism does: dismally. Contrary to Wegscheider-Cruse's claim, and as we learned in Chapter 8, "Insurance companies see the dismal recovery rates and have severely reduced monies for what they now know is fundamentally ineffective treatment." They see it for the snake oil that it is. What's more, laws passed in 1996 ended all Social Security payments for people with the "primary diseases" of alcohol/drug addiction and codependency. No disease, no money.

Victimhood Again

Wegscheider-Cruse labels 96% of the population "diseased." And they all need to be "in recovery" (yet they'll never recover). Her codependency concepts fit nicely with the victim mentality exhibited by many new agers: "I'm an emotionally scarred victim of my dysfunctional family," can be heard echoing throughout the rooms of CODA, Al-Anon, and ACOA meetings. As we saw in Chapter 8, victims need to blame their present-day dilemmas on outside forces, especially their repressive, crazy parents and bad childhoods. You don't.

ACOA (Adult Children Of Alcoholics) members actually believe that their adulthood troubles—insecurities, phobias, abandonment issues, weight problems, attracting inappropriate partners, compulsions, and addictions—are all consequences of their dysfunctional upbringings or bad genes. For them, blaming is a lot easier than living in the here and now, and taking responsibility for their lives and happiness. No wonder they label themselves Adult Children. They blame everything on mom and dad, or mom and dad's addictive diseases.

Sadly, children often do suffer horrific ordeals. But there are distinct differences between getting a zit on prom night, the chaos of boozed-up parents, and the trauma of pedophilia. But people do survive even very traumatic childhood experiences and often go on to lead happy, productive lives. Surviving a bad experience is very different from joining the ranks of the walking wounded, who wear their victimhood into adult life as a badge of honor. Like AA, ACOA is filled with vulnerable people who are ripe for the sales pitch of recruitment-minded groupers. The recovery merry-go-round swallows up "adult children" unmercifully, too.

The point is that 96% of us would be drafted into the codependency cartel if Sharon Wegscheider-Cruse, Anne Wilson Schaef, Joe Klaas, and their RGM comrades could write the script. Fortunately, they can't. Instead, you can write your own script. Title it "Never Was, and Never Will Be Codependently Diseased." You are incredibly resilient and possess great strength of mind and spirit, no matter what befell you earlier in life.

I'm surprised Wegscheider-Cruse didn't diagnose people with brown eyes as codependent. Her claim that 96% of us are diseased covers just about everyone. And if such a figure were true, the dysfunctional behavior Wegscheider-Cruse speaks of would be normal. Do you really believe that nearly all of us suffer from a "primary disease" that requires treatment and 12-step recovery?

Fortunately, the 12-step "revolution" peaked over a decade ago, and is now on a downhill slide. (Yes, many 12 steppers actually refer to their reactionary religious crusade as a "revolution.") But the RGM is still very powerful. And you'll still hear a lot about "the disease of codependency."

You need to discover a few things the codependency cartel can't give you. For one, the truth about your "disease." Let's see how diseased you really are.

Diagnosing and Treating Your "Disease"

The codependency cartel exploits the legitimate concerns of the family and friends of substance abusers to funnel more people into the recovery group movement. A starting point in the recovery process has you, the pigeon, pondering the difference between caring for, rather than about, someone. The cartel then categorizes your self-defeating learned behaviors as disease symptoms, and they affix all sorts of victim labels to you.

Check out this list taken from merry-go-round operator Earnie Larsen's book, *Stage II Recovery*. It describes the categories and symptoms of the "disease of codependency"—and these are only some of the symptoms that Larsen lists:

People-Pleaser
I have trouble saying no even when I know I should.
I often say, "It doesn't mater," when it really does.
I seldom feel angry but often feel hurt. . . .

Caretaker
Sometimes I wonder why so many people lean on me without being sensitive to my needs to lean once in a while.
I find it easier to take care of others than to take care of myself.
I never have enough time to accomplish all my tasks. . . .

Workaholic
> I rarely feel that I accomplish enough.
> It seems to me that people are in my way quite often.
> I spend more time, energy, and effort on projects than on relationships. . . .

Martyr
> I feel I have terrible luck.
> My first impulse is to say no when something fun comes up.
> When life runs smooth for a while, I begin to anticipate disaster.

Perfectionist
> I am often amazed at the incompetence of others.
> I can't stand it when things are out of place.
> I worry a lot about why I haven't done better. . . .

Tap Dancer
> I find it difficult or impossible to tell anyone the whole truth.
> I would rather end a primary relationship than make a binding commitment.
> I have an abiding fear of being "caught" or "cornered." . . .

So, did you find yourself in the above list? How should you label yourself? Perhaps you fit into more than one category. Perhaps you fit into all of the categories. Whatever your level of "disease" (and given the inclusiveness of the above list, you *are* diseased) there's a codependency club just for you.

Counseled with Colloquialisms

Doing some of the things on the above list is common. But what if you do many of them? If you bypass the insults to your intelligence and common sense, sponsors and other codependency truth keepers will "counsel" you. In step-talk, you'll hear:

> Welcome to Al-Anon, where "Easy does it" is our motto. Share our "experience, strength and hope." Here, you will "live and let live." You will "practice an attitude of gratitude" as you follow our lead and "stick with the winners."
> When you "KISS—Keep It Simple Stupid," you will be amazed. "Get out of the drivers seat." "Let go and let God," we always say.

"Turn it over" to your Higher Power. But be warned, "If you turn it over and don't let go of it, you'll be upside down." It's time to "count your blessings" and "come to believe," like we do. You see, "there is no magic in recovery, only miracles."

We in Al-Anon remind you to ask yourself, "If God seems far away, who moved?" Therefore, don't despair, because "fear is the darkroom where negatives are developed" and your loved one's "road to sobriety is a simple journey for confused people with a complicated disease." And never forget, "the will of God will never take you where the grace of God will not protect you." Our "faith is not belief without proof, but trust without reservation." For heaven's sake, though, don't get smug. "When your head begins to swell your mind stops growing." So, "have a good day unless of course you have made other plans" and "keep coming back-it works if you work it." Oh, and keep this in mind, "We are only as sick as our secrets" and, God knows, "some of us are sicker than others." (All quotes are common 12-step slogans)

Such wisdom! Except for having an addicted loved one, you're no different from people without this "disease" of codependency.

Still, dealing with an addicted loved one is no picnic. It does have you running the gamut of emotions. If you seek professional counseling, codependency therapists will begin analyzing your emotional disturbances while pushing you into Al-Anon, ACOA, Alateen, or CODA, and then monitoring your "progress." If you fall into this trap, your counseling and recovery will entail a laundry list of negatives that need to be sorted, one painful feeling at time: anger; anxiety; disappointment; hostility; humiliation; hurt; inadequacy; insecurity; isolation; loneliness; resentment; self-blame; worry.

Your "therapy" can last for years and your "recovery" will never end. Still, you need to purge the hurtful emotions you have tolerated but despised all these years. Surely, your codependency counselors know what's best for you. As actress Claire Danes tells it, "You don't realize how useful a therapist is until you see one and discover you have more problems than you ever dreamed of." And as if you haven't endured enough, they have another burden to lay on you.

The Cruelest Trick: "Enabling"

If you're in a relationship with an addict, addiction is an inescapable part of your life. It dominates in more ways than you can describe, let alone want to remember. The hardships you endure trying to hold things together, while your loved one is "out there," oblivious to the realities you are facing, is cruel and unusual punishment. Even if your loved one quits, arrogant, inconsiderate drinkers can be arrogant, inconsiderate non-drinkers. Family and friends, wives especially, often face incredibly belittling put-downs and nasty comments. Such debasement is never easy to take.

The truth is, you were hurt. You were let down by someone you love. The cartel exploits your pain using a cruel trick designed to convince you of your codependency. Did you know that you are the person responsible for allowing your loved one's addiction? Did you know that you are blocking his or her recovery, and that by codependently loving, you are destroying? Did you know that you are an addiction-breeding enabler? Your need to love and to be loved has distorted your mind to the point of disease. For your own selfish and sick reasons, you would rather have him or her around drunk than not at all. In other words, your "sickness" is allowing your loved one's "sickness" to continue.

But calling your caring behavior "sickness" is what's sick.

Remember Bill and Hillary? Did Hillary enable Bill, or was his behavior his responsibility? "Enabling" says that you fostered your loved one's addictive behavior. Discovery says that the addictive behavior of another is his or her own affair. Whether someone decides to have a fling, run for the Senate, or chug a pint of gin, *they* are responsible for what they do—not you. In other words, you just happen to care about someone who would have found a way to feed his or her addiction with or without your "enabling."

The skewed concept of enabling tells addicts that they are powerless over their behavior, and therefore not responsible for it, yet it tells those who are not engaging in the addictive behavior that they are responsible for the addictive behavior of others. This not only snares non-addicts into 12-step programs, but it keeps addicts dependent on others to sober them up and keep them that way. If someone doesn't step in to stop the addict, then he/she/they are "enabling." Indeed, such American institutions as the motion picture industry and Major League Baseball are labeled enablers. Why? Remember Robert Downey Jr. and Darryl Strawberry? By "codependently" helping them, film and MLB bigwigs are "allowing" their golden boys' addictions to thrive. Perish the thought that Robert and Darryl are responsible for their behavior.

But aren't we dealing with a "family disease?" Don't "enablers" have to do their part in recovery? Your "part" has nothing to do with bearing responsibility for the Parasite-driven, pleasure-seeking addictive behavior of another. Even if you enjoyed an occasional cocktail with your loved one in the past, you drank sensibly, and he or she didn't. Stop beating yourself up. Based on what you were facing, you probably behaved reasonably by covering up and making excuses for your addicted loved one. After all, there was much at stake: careers, relationships, children, finances, health, even life and death. Yet, the codependency cartel labels such reasonable behavior as diseased.

Still, let's face it: your behavior is not getting the results you want. And dealing with your loved one's addiction has you on an emotional roller coaster. This doesn't make you diseased, emotionally feeble or a candidate for lifelong recovery. Unfortunately for you, the codependency cartel doesn't see it that way. Let's tap into some heightened perception and discover what's really going on.

You Were Conned

As we saw in Chapter 6, addicts and alcoholics lie. They lie to get what they want and need. You have been lied to. You've been played like a well-worn violin. When you bailed him or her out (who wouldn't for someone they love?) your Parasite-driven con (wo)man was deftly pulling your strings. With the survival-minded Parasite in control, your addicted loved one exploited your help. This doesn't make you a diseased, codependent enabler. You're a fallible human being and you were conned!

You probably don't feel much better knowing you were taken advantage of, but you can do something about that; at the least you can do your best to avoid it in the future. You can't do much about your supposed "codependency" except let the cartel con you a second time.

There is a worldwide desire to be understood, to love, and to be loved. The codependency cartel considers this natural desire pathological. What is an "enabling codependent" to do? You could detach and become indifferent, but that's not in your character, nor is it a very satisfying way to live. Let's try something different.

Emotional Security and Self-Reliance

The codependency cartel would cease to exist if people developed emotional security. The cartel doesn't want you to know this. I do. Virtually all recovery groups focus on your emotional problems *ad nauseam*. Your peers evaluate your codependent behavior, which supposedly helps you identify your emotional blind spots. Pie charts, like The Feelings Wheel discussed in Chapter 4, track your ever-elusive, mixed-up emotions. People fill therapists' couches needing to "sort their feelings." There are even Emotions Anonymous recovery groups. Emotions are big business, and the codependency cartel clearly exploits emotional insecurity.

Emotional insecurity is a self-defeating proclivity toward clinging to the present at any cost. It's a desperate bid to remain in the comfort zone of what you know, no matter how uncomfortable. Battered Woman's Syndrome, dead-end jobs, and enduring both addictive relationships and ineffective recovery programs are examples. Relying on friends, a spouse, family or recovery groups to provide you with happiness and validate your judgments is an emotional crutch. A major problem with it is that it leaves you vulnerable, dependent on others.

Emotional security, in contrast, means trusting your own judgments and taking personal responsibility for your happiness and well-being. It hinges on self-reliance: knowing your worth, thinking for yourself, and having confidence in your abilities and personal resources. Abdicating self-reliance keeps you dependent on the codependency cartel. It keeps you stewing in the uncertainty, resentments, and self-pity that self-reliance alleviates.

All 12-step organizations provide a pre-packaged belief system. As the AA slogan, "Utilize, don't analyze" implies, everything is laid out for you. This is most disempowering because you don't need to think for yourself, indeed, you're not supposed to ("Let go and let God," "Your best thinking got you here"); instead of standing on your own two feet, you need The Program to function. You've traded one dependency for another.

None of this means you must become an island. Certainly, you are free to have friends and advisors. But when you need a meeting, or have to check with your sponsor, don't expect freedom from the codependency cartel any time soon. Emotional security, self-reliance, and independent thinking are liberating virtues. The codependency cartel/RGM considers them vices.

Discover Security Now

To be truly emotionally secure means cultivating a position of self-reliance that frees you from the bondage of others' judgments, approvals, and beliefs. It's like being an actor who says (and means it), "I never read the reviews." Whether it's thumbs up or down, he is free from the judgments, approvals, and beliefs of the reviewer. And you are free to start practicing this approach anytime you choose. How about now? You may think that this is a tall order, but it is not, especially when you consider the alternative: emotional bondage. Take this giant step toward independence. Work at it. With this freedom comes the power to boldly forge ahead, explore your options, make plans, set goals and take risks without the need for anyone's permission or approval. Above all, emotional security/self-reliance says that you are capable of discovering for yourself how best to live your life, and are capable of living it recovery free.

Taking Care of Number One

Recovery/codependency groups are not healthy places to spend your time. By their own standard, all members are diseased for life and must forever congregate to discuss their inadequacies of mind, body, and spirit. The past is senselessly rehashed through self-pitying war stories of abuse, neglect, and resentment. Pessimism abounds as you force yourself to try to identify, and not compare, with the woes of your recovering fellows. (All 12-step programs stress identifying with the thoughts and emotions of speakers. Comparisons are discouraged, but made.)

While it's comforting to know that you're not alone when you first meet other "codependents," associations based on counterfeit diseases and personal powerlessness grow old very quickly. You are left with superficial pals who only "like" you as long as you continue "working the program" and paying homage to spiritual guru Bill W. And we all like to be liked, don't we?

With slight modification for the codependency crowd, let me reaffirm something else from Chapter 4:

There is nothing anti-spiritual, blasphemous or criminal in questioning the value of any program, or the motives of its promoters, into which you have been thrust. If you are involved with Al-Anon, Alateen, CODA, ACOA, and the RGM of your own free will, and are happily where you want to be in the Wilsonian world of the perpetually recovering, please consider giving this book to someone less fortunate.

Are you where you want to be? Are you taking care of number one? Think of it this way: In an airplane, when the oxygen masks drop, adults are instructed to use them first. By taking care of themselves, they are better equipped to help children. Their first responsibility is their own well-being. Similarly, taking care of you is priority one. The last thing you need is the codependency cartel telling you how powerless and diseased you are. You'll be much more capable of taking care of yourself and your family when you breathe the oxygen of emotional security and self-reliance.

Goals And Options

Setting goals is a powerful way to create your future. It provides purpose and passion in daily life. Ask yourself, "What is preventing me from having what I really want?"—not what you need, but what you want. I can hear some of you now:

"My husband/wife is a drunk"
"My husband/wife won't let me"
"I'm a single mom"
"I don't have the knowledge"
"I don't have the skill"
"I'm not pretty/handsome enough"
"There's no time"
"I'm an ex-con"
"I'm too sick/tired/old/young"
"I'm unemployed"
"I'm on welfare"
"I'm afraid"

With emotional security, none of the above will hold you back. Let me remind you of something else from Chapter 4:

"Every time I clear up my problems and think it's time to move on with my life, a whole new set of problems seems to arise. Until one day it dawned on me, this is my life." Our friend certainly hit upon something. This was his life and he was free to live it, or have it lived for him.

This is your life. Are you living it, or is some manipulating puppeteer controlling you? Don't you want to pull your own strings? No matter what your circumstances, always remember: whenever you feel overwhelmed, whenever you feel like there is no way out, whenever you feel as if you're backed into a corner, you have lost sight of you options.

How do you discover your options? Whoever or whatever is pulling your strings can only continue to do so if you allow it. Eleanor Roosevelt said, "No one can insult you without your consent." And I say, "No one can hold me back without my consent." Who or what have you consented to? Perhaps your own fears of the future? I can't answer this for you. Identify the roadblocks in your path. Use the list above as a start. Your options will become clearer. Then you can make plans and set goals to overcome the roadblocks.

This reminds me of the award winning motion picture, "The Shawshank Redemption." Andy DuFreine, played by Tim Robbins, is falsely imprisoned for murdering his wife. In an emotional scene, Andy tells fellow inmate Red, played by Morgan Freeman, of a goal he has set. Not knowing how, when or if he would ever experience life outside the foreboding prison walls, Andy talks of a small sleepy town in Mexico. There he would live out the remainder of his days, open a small hotel, and enjoy the blue Pacific as his backyard.

You're not in a Hollywood movie; this is your life. But you can learn something from Andy. He set goals for himself, regardless of the fact that he was facing the roadblock of life in prison. Andy didn't know exactly how to achieve his goals or the rewards they might bring, but he set them anyway, mindful of the importance of having them. It was a means for creating his future. Equally important, Andy never lost sight of his options. He worked the prison system with a vigilant eye on finding a means of escape and the chance to reach his sleepy Mexican town.

You can do this too; you can set your own goals. And like Andy, you don't need to know every nuance of how to reach your goals when you set them. Do you think Bill Gates knew exactly how to build his multi-billion-dollar empire when he stared Microsoft from a garage? Start setting short-, mid-, and long-range goals, and take pleasure in the process of achieving them. To help you get started, let me remind you of something you discovered in Chapter 8:

> All human behavior, even the simplest everyday decision, is directed one way: to avoid pain and seek pleasure. We maximize pleasure when weighing similarly pleasant choices and minimize pain when confronted with similarly unpleasant choices The point is: pleasure over pain, comfort over discomfort.

Have you become comfortable in your discomfort? Has it become second nature to struggle with the familiar rather than forge ahead into the unknown? This is not to say that your current situations necessarily give you pleasure, but is the fear (of pain) of making a move keeping you in limbo? In other words, do you associate less pain with not changing and more pain with going for it? Look carefully at your situation. Do you really want discomfort, dissatisfaction forever? If you set goals and strive for them you might not get what you want; then again, you might. But if you don't set goals and just go with the familiar flow, you know exactly what you'll get. Is it what you really want? Here are some questions to help you decide:

"What will I miss out on if things remain the same?"
"What will it cost me if I don't change?"
"What will be the ultimate cost to my health, overall well-being and peace of mind if I continue on as I've been doing?"

Realizing that staying stuck creates more pain than changing does creates momentum and gives you a new, more productive perspective. This common-sense approach taps into your incredibly resilient human spirit, not some conjured-up RGM higher power. For added motivation, add your loved ones into the mix:

"What will it cost my family if I don't change?"
"What will my family miss out on if things remain the same?"
"What is the ultimate cost to my family's health, overall well-being and peace of mind if I continue on as I've been doing?"

Codependents don't ask themselves these self-motivating questions. You, on the other hand, do. (P.S.: Yes, Andy made it)

Break Up, Put Up, Shut Up, Make Up

Think long and hard about your relationship with your addicted loved one. Whether you want to continue with it is an intensely personal decision, and your best counsel will not come from world-weary groupers who are self-absorbed with their own codependency issues. Stick with family and trusted friends who love you for what you are, not for what the codependency cartel wants you to become: a Bill Wilson groupie. (And please realize that they'll toss you away like a hot rock the instant you stop toeing the 12-step line. "Friendships" in 12-step groups are highly contingent on conformity—they don't "love" you for who you are, but for the words you mouth.)

Be A Genius: Prepare

Emerson said, "People only see what they are prepared to see." Throughout this book, I've spoken of developing heightened perception to help you "see" and think things through. Now let's use heightened perception to better manage your life. Living in an addictive household means preparation and making plans. It means self-reliance. Should you break up, put up, shut up, or make up? First, you should make plans that reflect what you might need to do to take care of yourself. Study this 16-point list. Be prepared.

Self-Reliance Planning List for Those Living with Addicts

1. Evaluate your present home situation.
2. Should your addicted loved one leave, can you afford to maintain your house or apartment? For how long? Will he or she contribute? Can you rely on it?
3. Find a place to live should you decide to leave.
4. Open your own savings and checking accounts.
5. Establish or maintain credit.
6. Find work (even part-time).
7. Have emergency numbers at your fingertips should domestic flare-ups warrant immediate action.
8. Seek out shelter locations and find out if they accommodate children.

9. Have dependable transportation or familiarize yourself with mass transit options.
10. Investigate day-care or baby-sitting options.
11. Explain the situation to children who are old enough to under stand. (They know things are not "right.")
12. Gather information regarding insurance policies, mortgages, rental agreements, mutual debt and other bills.
13. Manage your finances. Besides checking and savings accounts, are there retirement plans, pensions, stocks, bonds, mutual funds, etc.?
14. Consult with an attorney.
15. Clearly inform the addicted loved one of your plans and that they will be carried out should the situation not improve. (If the addict is violent, though, it probably would be better to do all of the above that apply—and leave, if necessary—in secret.)
16. Inform at least one relative or trusted friend of your plans.

No one knows your situation better than you do. Modify this list to suit your needs. Planning makes the difference between rash decision-making and reasoned responses. Your plans are your responsibility. Take that responsibility.

Preparing for the worst doesn't mean the worst will happen. Homeowners buy fire insurance, but, fortunately, most never need to exercise their policies. It's like having an insurance policy; it's reassuring to know that you have a plan just in case. And remember, plans should be flexible; you should adapt yours to life's ever-changing circumstances. No one is stopping you from making new plans should your addicted loved one quit for good. It is said that genius lies in preparation. Be a genius—prepare.

Doing Your Part

Earlier I stated that your part in your loved one's addiction doesn't include bearing responsibility for his or her Parasite-driven, pleasure-seeking behavior. So, what is your part?

What can you do? There are options. You can:

1. Do nothing and hope for the best.
2. End the relationship and go your separate ways.
3. Get "in recovery" in Al-Anon or some other codependency program.
4. Help yourself by helping your loved one discover how to quit booze/drugs for good.

Options 1, 2, and 3 need no explanation; the fourth one does. First be aware that this option requires work. But when your loved one responds to the message in this book, your task will: 1) be temporary; 2) be well worth your time and effort; and 3) lead to full-time discovery of what life has to offer.

Two quick points: 1) Drunks are not always drunk. You must capitalize on their lucid and perceptive moments. Intoxicated persons can't grasp new ideas, and some are violent. 2) Always keep in mind that conversations with your addicted loved one involves you, your loved one, and his or her Parasite.

You will not be conducting an intervention. As you know from Chapter 6, they are largely ineffective. Interventions are designed to intimidate addicts through guilt and shame. This only enrages The Parasite, destroying the chance for effective communication. Equally ineffective is presenting your loved one with a laundry list of misdeeds. He or she knows the list, backwards and forwards. Even blackouts are "remembered." Either your loved one has been told of his or her outrageous behavior, or chunks of missing yesterdays serve as disturbing reminders. If you truly want to help your addicted loved one, you must work around The Parasite. Then you can begin communicating constructively.

Identify The Booze/Drug Problem

"Tom (use loved one's name), drinking is nothing new to either of us, but it has created problems that neither of us anticipated when we toasted each other on our wedding day."

Without finger pointing, you've identified the booze problem. Now, state that you have something to say, and that you will say it without interruption. Assure your loved one that his or her responses are important to you and that you will listen when you have finished. And be alert. Your loved one's Parasite will be listening to every word.

The Set-Up

Show him or her the dual-mind cycle diagram (see page 93). Take the time to study it together. Here, conversation is necessary. But be sure to stay on the subject. Your loved one is painfully aware of his or her addiction. Odds are, he or she has tried many times and many methods to moderate or stop. Some will have attempted recovery through rehabs and AA. Acknowledge all attempts. In fact, acknowledge that you now know that his or her complaints about treatment and AA are valid. It's okay to admit that you were ignorant of the facts, but now you have them. Disclose the treatment-failure statistics and dismal recovery rates of AA. Your loved one will be curious and relieved to know that it's not they who have failed The Program, but The Program that failed them.

Tell your loved one that you've discovered something which goes beyond treatment and recovery. Make it clear that what you have to say does not involve AA, meetings, rehabs, sponsors, or higher powers. You're going to focus on addiction alone. No step-talk, no counseling. Show them this book and let them read the title. Even your loved one's Parasite will wonder what's in its pages.

(TIP: Invariably, addicts swear that they are capable of moderating. Your loved one will be thinking, "I know I can cut back if I try." So, bring up the subject. Ask why they haven't done so already, if they "know" they can moderate. You can't force your loved one to quit his or her addiction. You can inform them of something you've learned that will empower them to quit now and for good. This gets your loved one thinking, which puts the first chink in The Parasite's armor.)

Give your loved one an overview of what you've learned in this book regarding the recovery group movement, the addiction treatment industry, and especially the recovery merry-go-round and its operators and riders. Reveal the Catch-22 in AA's concept of powerlessness. Expose alcoholism/addiction as the artificial diseases of the RGM and ATI. Make clear the lunacy in the mass prescribing of Bill Wilson's teachings to overcome it. Mention Charlie from Chapter 2, and that you now know the nightmare of merry-go-round recovery. Highlight whatever is relevant to you and your loved one.

The Pitch

Focus on the dual-mind cycle of addiction. Reinforce in your loved one the belief that he or she is not powerless, but has been listening to the "I want it," "Gotta have it" self-talk of addiction. Introduce The Parasite. Perform one Parasite-awareness exercise. Instruct your loved one to state aloud, "I will never drink booze again," and then listen. He or she will immediately "hear" the Parasite's self-talk: "I can't say never," "I can't predict the future." Explain that this has always been the problem. The Parasite is in charge, and when it says "Drink," your loved one listens and obeys. Stress the dual-mind cycle of addiction again.

But you have great news. You've learned of the techniques used by countless people who successfully beat this Parasite and knocked off booze and other addictions for good.

And it's all in this book.

The Follow Through

The ball is now in your loved one's court. Listen to his or her comments. You'll hear an eclectic mix, some from the heart, most from The Parasite. Don't be conned. At this point, most of what you'll hear is Parasite panic. Expect it. Don't waste your time debating with a pest. Besides, you have a trump card to play.

Before this initial conversation ends, let your loved one know that you have made some serious plans. Be honest. Let your loved one know that you're preparing to go it alone: "I do love you, and I want us to overcome this together. However, I've found a place for the kids and I to live, and I've contacted a lawyer about this whole mess. I'm putting our finances in order and have opened a bank account for myself. My plans are in motion. How they pan out depends on what you decide." However he or she decides, you'll soon be past one of the biggest roadblocks you'll ever face.

Hand this book to your loved one. Show him or her that the techniques you spoke of are clearly spelled out. Give him or her a few days to read and digest it. Make yourself available for discussions and keep an open ear for The Parasite. Before long, you'll know whether your loved one is serious about rebuilding your relationship and quitting booze for good. Then you'll know what options to consider, what plans to implement, what goals to set, and how to proceed. This is your future. Good luck.

A word of caution. Be very skeptical if after reading this book your loved one announces he or she needs "treatment" and the AA recovery package. Remember, The Parasite loves AA's never-quit-for-good disease recovery program. It's fond of addiction treatment with its talk of relapse triggers, H.A.L.T., enablers, and aftercare. If your loved one is looking for religion or spirituality, remind him or her that God will still be around when they quit for good.

On The Road Again

The late CBS broadcaster Charles Kuralt once spoke at a Skidmore College commencement. Kuralt must have learned something in his many years "On The Road." During his address, he urged the graduates to think for themselves, become emotionally secure and self-reliant:

> Great things are not accomplished by those who yield to trends and fads and popular opinion. Great things are not accomplished by teams, no matter what you have heard. They are accomplished by individuals who take untraveled roads.

Yielding to the opinion that codependency is an incurable disease does not make it so. No empirical evidence supports such a claim, yet the trend toward treatment and recovery for this non-disease is still epidemic. Fortunately, this fad is showing signs of fading away, but it's still strong. While America's insurance companies have wised up, the public hasn't (yet). But if you think of codependency the way I explained alcoholism in Chapter 6, you'll see why emotional security, self-reliance, preparation, weighing your options, and setting goals will help you create your future, not be stuck "in recovery" for the rest of your life.

If codependency is real, and you exhibit the described characteristics, wouldn't it be in your best interest to learn how to overcome it? If it's not a chronic disease, and you exhibit the described characteristics, wouldn't it still be in your best interest to learn how to overcome it? Whether or not it's a disease, the codependency cartel will never teach you to overcome it, only endure it while "recovering" and praying for a miracle.

Al-Anon, Alateen, CODA, and ACOA minister to the "family disease of codependency." These ministries boil down to Bill Wilson conversion mills. And for most troubled families, this heavily traveled road is not particularly helpful. Take this opportunity to create and discover the life you've always envisioned. Take the untraveled road and you'll accomplish great things.

And more great things are on the way. You and all the newly self-discovered are about to graduate. The next chapter celebrates your commencement into the liberating world of people who know how to: 1) quit addictions and overcome their adversities; 2) live recovery free; and 3) discover for the rest of their lives. As Paul McCartney sings in Blackbird: "Take these broken wings and learn to fly. All your life, you were only waiting for this moment to arise. You were only waiting for this moment to be free."

Chapter 14

Ready to Rock

"Go confidently in the direction of your dreams.
Live the life you have imagined."
—Henry David Thoreau

"Put me in coach. I'm ready to play, today."
—John Fogerty

Born of long frustration and a passion for self-determination, the 13 original colonies issued the Declaration of Independence July 4, 1776. The Declaration listed the colonists' grievances against tyranny. It speaks of the inalienable rights of all men. Among these is the right to life, liberty, and the pursuit of happiness. You've just made a similar declaration—a declaration of freedom from addiction, recovery, and the tyranny of an oppressive recovery group movement.

Look at your addiction-busting discoveries:

- Heightened Perception
- The Dual Mind Cycle of Addiction
- The Parasite & Parasite Panic
- Translation
- Commitment
- P.A.W.N.

Discovery also gives you two priceless gifts the recovery group movement cannot: freedom and time. No more midnight calls to sponsors, no more "working the program," no more bouncing from meeting to meeting, from counselor to therapist. You can now live your own life. To that end, I urge you to use some of your newfound time to set goals—short, mid, and long range. Goals are a key to creating your recovery-free future.

But an old nemesis wants to scuttle your goals: The Parasite has one last grandstand play. It echoes RGM teachings from your recovering past. Remember, The Parasite loves AA's concept of power-lessness. It wants to walk you down merry-go-round lane, believing that eventually you'll go running for the booze. Fear not. As you discovered with P.A.W.N., your awareness will make this final Parasite plot easy to neutralize.

Let's expose those old teachings The Parasite uses against you—then you'll be ready to rock.

The Goal-Keepers

Goal-keepers are merry-go-round operators who don't want you to manage your own life. Like hockey goalies, they try to block you from reaching your goals—more accurately, they try to block you from even setting goals. In their one-day-at-a-time sobriety world, goals violate the serenity of living in the moment. They lead to frustration, despair, and back to the bottle. The Parasite dredges up this foolishness to shake your confidence. Let's examine this RGM belief.

The future is unknowable. No matter what you plan, the possibility of failure exists. Goal-keepers cannot accept the *possibility* of failure so they *predict* it. Recall Bill Wilson's first step: "We admitted we were powerless over alcohol that our lives had become unmanageable."

It's very important to note that this step applies not just to booze, but to our whole lives. Placing themselves in a state of perpetual helplessness, 12-steppers have no choice but to petition higher powers for daily direction—indeed, if they're consistent, minute-by-minute and second-by-second direction. And since sobriety only lasts for 24-hour clips, long-range plans are dubious endeavors. Setting goals then, only proves what a powerless, unmanageable life you lead. How? Once again, the RGM recruitment handbook, *The 12 Steps To Happiness*, clarifies, with stark pessimism, its "no goals allowed" position:

> All you have to do to convince yourself that you are powerless is set a goal with all its rewards specified in detail. You will never achieve it exactly the way you planned. The joy of even partly attaining such a goal will be diluted by the frustrating way of life required to try to accomplish a goal. People who set goals live in the past when they set them and in the future when they hope to attain them. They forget how to live in the now at all. So by the time they get to any goal they never arrive satisfied at a destination. . . .

[L]ive only in the present with no goals at all—the second half of the First Step is to admit that our lives have become unmanageable. How could we possibly plan ahead enough to achieve goals unless we are planning our own future? In other words, he who plans goals is obviously still trying to manage his life. As long as we think we can do that, we will be unable to admit we cannot.

With this "why bother?" attitude, it's no wonder only 3% of AA members achieve any type of lasting sobriety. "Dare to be great!" "Aim high!" But not in the RGM. Expect nothing, and you won't be disappointed. Your inability to unerringly detail and plan goals proves how powerless you are and unmanageable your life is. And the goal keepers expect you to accept this—unquestioningly. But is this any way to live? Damn accepting personal powerlessness! Will this abandonment of self-direction lead to sobriety, let alone, happiness?

Even if you decide to reclaim your life, these convoluted teachings sit in your subconscious waiting for The Parasite to dredge them up. You can see why I've stressed honing your heightened perception skills. The RGM's influence lingers long after you leave the fold.

Invariably, The Parasite reverts to an old standby: attacking your self-esteem. We addressed this in Chapter 8, where you discarded conditional self-esteem and replaced it with unconditional self-acceptance. Still, The Parasite will try. If you set goals and fail, you'll be "driven" to drink, because you feel bad. If you succeed, you'll again be "driven" to drink, because you'll want to celebrate. If you don't set any goals, you'll be forlornly "driven" to drink, because you've stagnated.

Of course, nothing can "drive" you to drink. Since you've adopted self-acceptance (instead of conditional self-esteem, based on self-rating), you have nothing to fear. However, listen for the parasitic fear-mongering that holds you back from confidently pursuing your dreams. It can take the form of past conversations with group members, sponsors, or counselors, or come from the Big Book or other RGM literature.

You won't hear the classic, "I want it, gotta have it" in self-sabotaging RGM self-messages. Listen now for self-talk that suggests powerlessness and unmanageability. Then use translation for an empowering awareness shift. For example:

"I don't have the knowledge" becomes
"The Parasite wants me to remain ignorant."

"I don't have the skill" becomes
"The Parasite wants me to remain inept."

"I don't have the time" becomes
"The Parasite wants me to procrastinate."

"I'm afraid" becomes
"The Parasite wants me to remain fearful."

Did you ever take music lessons? Have you ever tried out for a team or auditioned for a show? Have you applied for a job or saved money to buy a car or house? Did you ever set out to earn a degree, start a business, write a book, climb a mountain, cook a great meal, run a marathon, learn a new language, or get online? According to the goal-keepers, you will never achieve any of these goals exactly, and even the joy of attaining them partly is "diluted by the frustrating way of life required to accomplish it." Following the goal-keeper's warped logic, we should ban Little League and Peewee football. Those poor frustrated kids can't all win the championship—and we know what frustration leads to. And for those who do win, receiving their coveted trophies will never be achieved exactly the way they imagined. Like you, those kids need to be working a good program —with no other goals in sight.

Do you see how goal-keepers sabotage your ambition by tying it into their twisted concept, "disease of relapse?" Just as H.A.L.T. supposedly leads to the bottle, goals do, too.

In fact, you must add goals to your lengthy list of relapse triggers. Like a child, the RGM blames everything but the bad decisions of its members for relapse. Really. The RGM handbook, *12-Steps to Happiness* makes this explicit:

> If we are powerless and cannot manage our own lives, then we no longer have to take the blame for our mistakes, unless we continue to try to manage our own lives. If we continue to try we must be insane.

Recognize these destructive RGM teachings and don't allow them to interfere with your discovery—your future. This is your life to create, not the goal-keepers' to misdirect.

The Goal-Keepers' Spin

Goal-keepers spin a familiar tale with their "no goals" policy: by allowing Higher Powers to guide you, you can accept success if it comes to you from "outside" yourself. Again, from *12-Steps to Happiness:*

> There is no way we can achieve success if we cannot learn to manage our own lives. But we can accept success if it comes to us from outside of ourselves. Yet before we can even consider accepting a fate determined by such an outside force, we must somehow have it irrefutably proven that indeed our lives have become unmanageable and that we will never learn how to manage them.

Lives that have *become* unmanageable indicate that they *were* manageable. Start managing yours again. Thwart the goal-keepers' mission to convince you that your life is out of control and that you can't achieve anything without "outside forces" determining your fate.

Did Karol Wojtyla set out to become Pope John Paul II? I doubt it. John Paul II is an example of a person accepting success via "outside forces." And that's great for the pope, but few of us will be up for the papacy any time soon. The goal-keepers' "no goal" policy is another contrivance to keep you vulnerable and obedient. Don't let The Parasite/AA use these tricks to hold you back.

Set Your Sights

When he first determined his goals, do you think Thomas Edison knew exactly how to develop the light bulb? Did Marconi know every circuit when he began work on his radio? Do you think Donald Trump knew every zoning ordinance on his way to the top? Didn't Martin Luther King Jr. have a dream?

Review the Goals and Options section in Chapter 13 and set some goals now. Write them down. Tape them to your refrigerator. Read them daily. Each day gives you new opportunities to pursue your desires. Take some chances. Don't be afraid.

Goals are stepping-stones toward creating your future. But don't feel that you have to know all your long-term goals this minute.

Short- and mid-range goals often develop into rewarding long-term commitments. In fact, give your long-term goals careful consideration. Ask yourself if they will add to your happiness. If you're not sure, experiment with doing different, new things. You'll develop a fresh perspective, which will help you decide what you want to do, and might spark interests in entirely new areas you'd like to pursue.

Here's a good tip: Be flexible. Be prepared to modify your plans as new information becomes available or as conditions change. There's no fixed blueprint. That's what keeps things fresh and exciting. And on those days when it seems everything is going against you, taking baby steps makes sense. Set mini-goals. Map out what you need to accomplish for the day. Do what you can to satisfy your immediate needs. You're not superhuman and tomorrow is another day. Remember—be flexible.

Goals are for your own enjoyment and the benefit of others. Think about it. An Internet business you probably know, Amazon.com, was the brainchild of Jeff Bezos. While rewarding to him personally, Jeff's goals have helped millions by creating jobs and making "point and click" on-line shopping a breeze—and it all began when he set short-, mid- and long-range goals.

The RGM blocks you and your family from the success goals can bring. You will never know what could have been if you place yourself in their straitjacket. If ignorance is bliss, than 12-step goal-keepers want you to be ecstatically ignorant. It's up to you to edit-out The Parasite's and RGM's memory tapes. Otherwise, you'll never live up to your potential. You'll deprive yourself, your family and, who knows, maybe the world of the things you might have accomplished. Big or small, achieved in full or part, your goals keep you rockin'.

The RGM just doesn't get it. Reaching exact goals was never the point. Rather, it's the person you become along the way and the continuing sense of fulfillment inherent to your discovery journey that provides the deepest satisfaction. Whatever comes from outside forces is gravy.

Darryl's Identity

How you define yourself affects your thinking and behavior. "Your Honor, I'm a drug addict. That's what I am. I go out looking for drugs to get high." This is what Darryl Strawberry said to a Florida judge. Recently, the former baseball star broke probation for _ne 1 ~·rth time. He didn't return to the court-ordered drug treatment facility where he was living under house arrest.

Picked up at the facility by a recovering friend, Darryl never made it to his meeting that night. His fellow AAer began smoking crack in the car. Darryl the addict "had" to participate. "Something snapped," said Strawberry. He was "powerless," and true to his self-description, he went "out looking for drugs to get high."

After multiple rehab treatments, and at the direction of his addiction counselors, Darryl identifies himself as a drug addict. Stripped away are his empowering identities of father, husband, and gifted baseball slugger; he's a drug addict first. That's his identity. Darryl lives up to it (more accurately, he lives down to it). And the RGM wants him to maintain it as his primary identity for the rest of his life.

Flashback to Chapter 2:

> You are much more than an addiction. The RGM doesn't want you to know that. I do. Forever identifying yourself as the victim of mythical diseases keeps you spinning on the recovery merry-go-round: "My name is Bob, and I'm an alcoholic," "My name is Brenda, and I'm an addict." Start empowering yourself no matter what your circumstances. Begin now and stop the label game. You don't have to brand yourself a recovering anything just because the RGM says so. Never forget, you are always a worthwhile human being much bigger than any addiction.

Shortly after Strawberry's four-day binge, a friend visited him and told a newspaper, "He said he was doing very well in rehab and was trying very hard, but the urge for the drug is too much for his willpower. His head snaps, his brain goes into the 'I want drugs' mode."

Sound familiar? Remember the dual-mind cycle of addiction? You understand it. With heightened perception, you recognize Parasite panic. And you know how to translate The Parasite's messages: "I want drugs" becomes "The Parasite wants drugs." You know how to separate from the parasitic self-talk, giving yourself the opportunity to stop, think, and apply P.A.W.N. You've made The Commitment.

Darryl knows none of this. Indeed, treatment taught him that his head-snapping "I want drugs" self-talk was too much for his willpower, and so he predictably failed, relapsed. He was told that only a Higher Power could save him, and for some reason his Higher Power abandoned him in his time of need. Darryl and other "recovering" people need to know that staying off booze and other drugs is not so much a matter of willpower as it is a matter of acting in their own best interests. As one of the self-discovered, you now know this.

Strawberry's battle with colon cancer cannot be ignored. He has said that the combination of rehab and chemotherapy has worn down his willpower. In the eyes of the RGM, he's fighting two diseases. If Darryl had been taught how to quit his addiction for good when he first sought "treatment" some ten years ago, he wouldn't be dealing with chemotherapy and drug rehab today. He could concentrate on beating his real disease in a healthy manner benefitting himself and his family. Poor Darryl is a long-time rider on the recovery merry-go-round "Treatment Works" campaign.

Darryl abided by the RGM's instructions to identify himself— before anything else—as an addict. Darryl believes himself to be a drug addict with a permanent problem, and he has acted accordingly. Allowing him to perceive himself as a fallible person with a temporary addiction is unfathomable to the RGM. They fear that "recovering" people will "forget" that they cannot use booze/drugs safely. The problem with this is that the daily self-identification with problem behaviors (past or present) preached by the RGM has produced nothing but the relapse-repent-contemplate cycle for the vast majority of people who come to the RGM for what passes for help. Instead of identifying themselves with their problems—forever—they need to discover what you have: how to quit booze/drugs for good and drop the fatalistic "addict for life" persona.

With the Scarlet Letter approach to addiction, your identity centers on your use of alcohol and other drugs. As a lifelong recovering addict or recovering alcoholic, you always use booze or drugs to label yourself. It's time to create your own identity.

Create Your Own Identity

Review the Emotional Security and Self-Reliance section of the last chapter. It applies to everyone. Without the bondage of others' approval, you are free to define yourself. This is the first step in carving out your own identity.

People define themselves in various ways: by profession ("I'm a doctor"); by family ties ("I'm an uncle"); by their looks ("I'm pretty"); by their religion ("I'm Catholic"); by their emotions ("I'm shy"). And it's not surprising that people act in accord with the way they define themselves. By definition, alcoholics drink alcohol and drug addicts take drugs. It would be surprising if this damaging self-definition doesn't account in part for the astoundingly high relapse rates among members of 12-step groups. But you don't have to buy into the RGM's labels. Now that you have quit booze/drugs for good, the RGM can't hold you back.

The things you achieve don't necessarily reflect your true capabilities. They are more likely the result of your beliefs about who you are and how you identify yourself. But identifying yourself is not the same as labeling yourself. You'll be better equipped to reach your goals by including "emotionally secure" and "self-reliant" as part of your identity than by tagging yourself a powerless, incurable recovering alcoholic or drug addict.

Identify yourself in as many empowering and enjoyable ways possible: "I'm a little league coach, soccer mom, volunteer, movie fan, musician, health nut, gardener." You do many things and have numerous attributes on which to build.

Go beyond the limit of your own experiences. Don't restrict yourself only to what you already know. In other words, you may be single and earn your living as a computer programmer, but you can also identify yourself as an author if you're writing a book, or a great chef if that's your hobby. Nurture the identities that give you pleasure and a vision for your future. Dr. Wayne Dyer puts it this way, "Treat yourself as if you are already what you'd like to become." Doing this helps you focus on your goals and divorces you from the destructive, backward-looking identity: alcoholic/drug addict.

Even better, combine your new identity with enthusiastically talking about your goals, and you'll enjoy a secondary benefit—built-in motivation. By announcing to friends and family, "I'm writing a book," you prod yourself into action. Would you want to identify yourself as an aspiring author if you've only come up with a title? Declaring your ambition to others pushes you to make it happen. You'll want to make good on your declaration. You might even take a refresher course to hone your skills or learn anew.

Additionally, when you combine your identity with The Commitment, you become the best author, spouse, parent, student, teacher you can be who never drinks booze. Don't try to do this. Do it. In his bestseller, *How To Argue and Win Every Time*, attorney Gerry Spence tells an appropriate story:

A young buckaroo who had just been thrown from his horse, dusted off his pants and, embarrassed, came limping up to the old cowboy who had witnessed the kid's humiliation.

"Why didn't ya ride 'em?" the old cowboy asked.

"I tried," the kid said.

"Ya tried?" the old boy replied. "Ya see that steer over there?" (As most know, steers are castrated bulls. Their fate is to grow fat and be butchered.)

"Well, ya put that steer in a herd of young heifers and what's he gonna do? He's gonna try. That's all. Steers try. You ain't no steer, kid. Now go ride that horse." And the kid did.

Do it

Some will say that your projected identity is fantasy. Others will chide you for living in the future. Your identity reflects where you are now, and where you'd like to go. As you continue to discover, your identity matures. It adapts and changes; it's like going from high school to college and from college into the "real world." Remember, goal setting and planning are today's activities with an enthusiastic eye on tomorrow. This is something the RGM still doesn't get. But you do.

The Mirror Effect

Project your new identity with conviction and it will reflect back on you—it will affect how people treat you. For instance, most people avoid unsavory looking characters. Expensively dressed people get better service than average folks do in restaurants. And fast-talking salespeople inspire distrust. Essentially, you treat people according to the image they project and the way you identify them, and vice versa.

This mirror effect is very powerful. Be careful not to project images you don't want coming back to haunt you. If you wear the Scarlet A of "Recovering Alcoholic," people will see you as a person they must tiptoe around. Remember, most people have been conned into believing you're diseased and can relapse at any time. "Uh-oh, Uncle Steve is coming over, better hide the booze. Don't want to 'trigger' him."

Diseases create powerful images, which are hard to escape. Think of Ronald Reagan, Michael J. Fox, and Muhammad Ali. Sure, you know these men for their accomplishments, but their diseases overshadow them today. Their illnesses have become a large part of their identity.

The fact is, people treat you differently when they know you are "recovering" from abusing booze/drugs. Recovering alcoholics get endless apologies from embarrassed friends and family when they've innocently made the slightest reference to booze. You want proof? This hospital story reveals all:

Frank, and to his own chagrin, sadly, identifies himself as a recovering alcoholic. When sitting with his family in the waiting room while grandpa Joe was having open heart surgery, sister in-law, Mary, began feeling anxious, "I wish there were a bar in the hospital so we could all go for a drink." As if she had funneled drinks down his throat, Mary winces and apologizes to Frank for making such an inconsiderate "triggering" comment. After all, Frank is "recovering" from the RGM'S "incurable, progressive disease of spontaneous relapse." The stress of grandpa Joe's surgery is bad enough. Suggesting a booze break might push Frank over the edge.

Your mere presence (and your comments) have your family and friends monitoring their words and behavior. You don't need that.

Another ludicrous example of this type of behavior occurred when, after winning the 1999 World Series, the New York Yankees popped sparkling cider in lieu of the traditional champagne. They didn't want to "trigger" their "recovering" teammates. This thoughtful consideration actually reflected the RGM's and ATI's duping of tens of millions of Americans into believing that alcoholism is a disease characterized by spontaneous relapse. The Yankees' gesture really says to teammates, "We know you're powerless drunks. We won't drink in front of you because you'd be unable to stay on the wagon when your disease kicks in."

If the Yankees had celebrated with the real stuff, and Darryl, for example, had chosen to join in, they'd be blamed for "enabling" him. Darryl could have blamed his disease, and his addiction counselors would have used the incident to "prove" his powerlessness as they ushered him off to another rehab. If Darryl had discovered what you have in this book, his teammates could shower with champagne daily and he wouldn't blink—unless the bubbles got in his eyes.

You can't help what people already know about your addicted past, but you don't have to draw attention to yourself by wearing the

Scarlet A. Eventually, your friends and family will know that you have quit for good. And the more people quit for good, the more their families, friends, and society will recognize the silliness of the "recovering" identity. Take this opportunity to launch a powerful new identity. Lay it out for the world to see. Project it confidently and reap the rewards.

The Land of the Free

While the Declaration of Independence explained the reasons for wanting independence, The Constitution, and especially The Bill of Rights, is our national charter outlining our freedoms. Today, as a nation, we suffer egregious lack of freedoms under recovery group movement rule. Over one million of our fellow citizens are coerced annually, often by the government, into the RGM's religious indoctrination programs.

The bitter experiences suffered under tyranny spawned the principles that shaped our nation. So, the founding fathers placed a high premium on religious freedom. Several U.S. courts (including all four appeal-level courts that have heard cases) have ruled that Bill Wilson's AA fellowship is unequivocally religious, so let's set aside the "religious vs. spiritual" debate. AA is religious. Period. As yet, there is no national binding precedent stating that coercing people into this religious institution is unconstitutional. So, mass government- and employer-coerced religious indoctrination continues in "the land of the free."

We're still plagued with a monolithic institution whose program fails 97% of the people who try it. That's the reality. The First Amendment reads in part: "Congress shall make no law respecting the establishment of religion, or prohibit the free exercise thereof." The recovery group movement is free to establish its own "recovery" religion, and to lay down spiritual laws for its adherents. They should have this right. But they shouldn't have the right to suppress alternative forms of recovery, nor should they have the right to force people into their religious program. Put simply, that's tyrannical and unconstitutional.

The Brass Ring

Machiavelli observed, "Most people have eyes and can therefore see. However, few people have the ability to reason. Therefore appearances are everything." AA and the RGM appear legitimate. They appeal to the emotions; and because they emphasize style over substance, they seem to succeed.

I disagree, though, with Machiavelli on one point. Many people have the ability to reason, but few people have fully realized that ability. I've stressed heightened perception, awareness, and developing your capacity to think, reason and make the choices that are right for you. Cultivate your abilities. You can do it.

This book is about reclaiming the freedom that addictions take away and the RGM pretends to deliver. My objective has been to get you thinking and to help you free yourself from the bondage of addiction and recovery. Whether you agree with some or most of what I've said, I hope that you've discovered the power you command and how to put it to use. Nobody has the one best solution for everyone for beating booze and other drugs. But recovery group movement members have no respect for any views other than their own, and their appallingly low success rate does not justify this intolerance. Fortunately, you don't need them. I've presented you with a solid way out of addiction, and it's yours to take, no strings attached.

I hope I've answered many questions for you. If I've raised others or touched on ideas you wish were covered in more detail, great! This means you're thinking. Let it spur you to investigate options, search out solutions, and ask more questions. The answers are there. Just as I am discovering daily, so are you. In fact, I'm not the same person I was when I started writing this book. I've learned much about people, friendships, family, and myself, and that's affected me. I have new perspectives on persistence and patience, and have honed my emotional security and self-reliance skills. If I had listened to the naysayers, you wouldn't be reading this.

Once upon a time, everyone knew that the earth was flat and the sun revolved around it. Today, everyone knows that alcoholism, drug addiction and codependency are incurable diseases and that "treatment works." Sometime in the future, everyone will know that this fairytale isn't true, either. Until then, millions of vulnerable souls will desperately cling to fruitless recovery programs. They will struggle for years. Others will go to early graves, because no one ever told them of their treatment and recovery options. I'm telling you now, and I urge you to tell others. It really is a matter of life and death.

Goodbyes can be difficult. But you won't find it difficult saying goodbye to the recovery merry-go-round. You have discovered how to remain booze, other drug, and recovery free for the rest of your life. You are the architect of your own life. Design it. Create it. Share it. Live it. Discover It!

Go out and rock. You have grabbed the brass ring and jumped off The Recovery Merry-Go-Round.

Appendix A

Drugs Used to Treat Addictions

Antabuse (Disulfiram)

Antabuse is an alcohol abuse-deterrent medicine. It does not decrease the drive to drink alcohol. Instead, it makes you sicker than hell if you drink any time within *days* of taking it. Expect severe physical reactions if you drink alcohol while taking Antabuse. Among these reactions:

- Nausea
- Abdominal pain
- Flushing
- Extreme thirst
- Vomiting
- Chest pain
- Dizziness
- Difficult breathing
- Fast heartbeat
- Fainting
- Confusion
- Heart attack/death (rare)

Products containing alcohol such as perfumes, colognes, after-shave and mouthwash can and do trigger Antabuse reactions, as may foods containing alcohol, rum cake for example.

Using Antabuse sends a mixed message to The Parasite. While it shows a sincere desire to quit, it also tells The Parasite that you are still ambivalent over your future use of alcohol, and are not ready to say, "I'll never drink again." It is, however, an empowering step up from relying on the RGM's higher powers.

Marie's and Paul's (not real names) story shows that the prescribed dose of Antabuse needs careful monitoring: For about eight weeks, Marie administered the daily 250mg dose of Antabuse prescribed to her husband, Paul. One late afternoon the phone rang; Marie was shocked to hear slurred speech. Arrested for DUI, Paul was calling from jail. She knew her husband was taking Antabuse and both of them were well schooled as to the reactions he should have experienced upon the slightest use of alcohol. What Marie didn't know, but Paul had gambled on and figured out, is that for Antabuse to be effective, it needs to be at a high enough level in the body to almost totally shut down a liver enzyme called acetaldehyde dehydrogenase.

The prescribed 250mg did not sufficiently inhibit the enzyme in Paul's body. Consequently, he suffered no physical ill effects from consuming alcohol. A higher dose, possibly 375mg or even 500mg might have been necessary in Paul's case to sufficiently inhibit the enzyme.

Knowing that Antabuse is coursing through your system can be an excellent alcohol deterrent. But "forgetting" to take it for a few days tells The Parasite that you are in the clear for boozing—if you're still feeling ambivalent, you no longer have the chemical protection the drug gives you. Long-term use of Antabuse is not recommended. The side effects can be extreme:

• Blurred vision
• Dizziness
• Skin rash
• Labored breathing
• Irregular heartbeat
• Confusion
• Impotence
• Yellowing of skin or eyes
• Body odor
• General fatigue & drowsiness

Another concern is its toll on the liver, which may already be damaged through excessive alcohol abuse.

Antabuse therapy is a major decision for people who desire an alcohol-free life. But if you truly want to end your dependence on alcohol, it only postpones facing down The Parasite. While Antabuse gives you ammunition, self-discovery and heightened perception provide the arsenal.

Revia (Naltrexone Hydrochloride)

Manufactured by Dupont-Merck, Revia is an orally administered opiate antagonist. This means that it blocks the euphoric effects of drugs such as heroin, morphine, and codeine, and synthetic opiate drugs such as oxycodone, which is found in Percocet, Percodan, and Dilaudid. Interestingly, Revia also combats alcohol dependence. In placebo-controlled, double-blind trials, patients receiving Revia experienced less alcohol craving and lower relapse rates than patients who received a placebo. Revia use does not lead to physical or psychological dependence.

Unlike Antabuse, Revia won't produce violent physical reactions if you ingest alcohol while taking it. But, it has its own side effects:

• Nausea
• Headache
• Fatigue
• Insomnia
• Anxiety
• Depression
• Vomiting
• Nervousness
• Somnolence
• Dizziness

It can also damage the liver. Revia treatment typically involves taking 50mg once daily for up to twelve weeks. Your physician can prescribe Revia and monitor your progress, but the RGM's influence over the medical profession will likely have your doctor strongly recommending that an overall "treatment" plan based on AA/12-step participation accompany Revia therapy. This gives merry-go-round operators a 12-week indoctrination window.

Revia does its job by blocking the euphoric effects of opiates. Because of this, the risk of opiate overdose is considerable. Your panicky Parasite cries, "You won't feel anything. Maybe five Percocet will do the trick." But with knowledge of the dual-mind cycle and The Parasite, you will: 1) Translate the message: "The Parasite won't feel anything and wants me to take five Percocet"; 2) apply P.A.W.N.

and 3) Neutralize The Parasite. Then, Revia can be a stepping-stone to overcoming your ambivalence and making The Commitment.

Methadone

Fearing a shortage of pain relievers, German chemists synthesized methadone during World War II. Little did they realize the impact their invention would have in the following years. Methadone is not a cure for heroin addiction. It is a long-acting synthetic opiate used today primarily for heroin detoxification and maintenance programs. It shares most of heroin's physiological properties including sedation, labored breathing, and, most notably, addictive properties and possible death from overdose. Unlike the typical two-to-six-hour fix supplied by heroin and most other opiates, methadone's effects can last up to 24 hours.

For the past several decades, the government has supervised and sponsored programs that supply methadone free to heroin addicts. This gets the addict off the street and out of the criminal world, but actually deepens the addiction—maintenance programs tell addicts that they "need" to maintain an addiction. Even so, methadone maintenance proponents equate methadone maintenance to providing insulin to diabetics. They consider this a dependency on the drug (to promote wellness), not an addiction to the drug. What methadone advocates have trouble perceiving is that diabetics are concerned with controlling a *real* disease—diabetes. There is no disease of addiction for opiate addicts to control. What they do have is a body that needs detoxifying, and addictive behavior that they need to change.

Also, methadone withdrawal lasts longer than heroin withdrawal. Instead of feeling lousy for five or six days, you'll feel lousy for a few days longer. Fatal reactions to methadone withdrawal are possible, too. While the physical discomfort between withdrawing from methadone and heroin are similar, methadone's chemistry makes medically supervised detox your safest and wisest choice.

Methadone is administered orally, abating infection and communicable diseases such as HIV, because needles are not involved. You will not be "out of it" under methadone, but you will be dependent on it if not outright addicted to it.

Methadone is stored in the liver and bloodstream. Similar to time-release medicines, it slowly, as needed, passes to the brain where it fills waiting opiate receptors. Ideally, methadone maintenance should be a finite process. But tapering off to a "zero dose" and becoming drug free is the antithesis of methadone maintenance. Indeed, methadone maintenance becomes the addict's methadone lifestyle. While the drug allows addicts to function within society, they cannot, or will not, accept the notion of living life without the support of their synthetic crutch.

Methadone knows no bigger fan than The Parasite, because it keeps it fat and happy. But now perhaps you see a light at the end of the methadone tunnel. You are not powerless over heroin *or* methadone. If you're on it, re-evaluate your relationship with methadone maintenance if you want to master The Parasite. Freedom from addiction and recovery is yours to discover.

Don't sell yourself short.

Acomprosate

Acamprosate is another drug for combating alcohol addiction. Similar to Naltrexone, Acamprosate is an anti-craving medication that acts on the brain to help control the urge to drink. Used for years in Europe, the pill is under review by the FDA. Approval is expected in late 2002.

Buprenorphine

Buprenorphine is a new, under-the-tongue lozenge targeting the heroin addict. The drug acts like a gentler methadone, and is neither intoxicating nor dangerous at high doses. Reckitt Benckiser Pharmaceutical of Richmond, Va., has applied to market buprenorphine under the name Suboxone. Federal approval is expected soon.

Vaccines

Stimulants like cocaine and methamphetamine do not affect the brain as do the opiates or alcohol. Currently, there is no pill/medication/drug to "treat" these addictions. However, Yale University is developing a vaccine, which may block these drugs' effects for as long as six months at a time. The vaccine won't be available for at least several more years, as testing continues.

Conclusion

Drug therapies have proven useful for overcoming addiction. Unfortunately, a huge caveat accompanies the prescription: "Medications are only a small part of treatment. You must receive counseling and participate in on-going recovery through AA or another 12-step fellowship. Otherwise, the pills might as well be candy." This talk comes from merry-go-round operators. And it is false. How many FDA approved medications are you aware of that require a corresponding dose of Bill Wilson's teachings to be effective?

Drug treatments buy you time until you can master The Parasite and make The Commitment. Be wary if they keep you dependent and/or "recovering." Remember, you call the shots, not the RGM, not the ATI, and not The Parasite. Good luck.

Appendix B

Abstinence-Based Alternatives to 12-Step Programs

A recent Gallup poll showed (once again) that most individuals quit serious additions without counselors, programs, or treatment:

People are about 10 times more likely to change on their own as with the help of doctors (physicians), therapists, or self-help groups. Professional help had surprisingly little to do with important life changes, even health-related ones. Doctors helped people change only 3% of the time, while psychologists and psychiatrists, self-help groups and religious counselors got the credit even less often. Support was much more likely to come from friends (14%), parents, children, or siblings (21%), or a spouse, boyfriend, or girlfriend (29%). And 30% of the time, people simply did what they had to do on their own, often with striking success.

As I've stressed throughout this book, recovery programs are not necessary to discover how to quit and stay quit. But for those who are interested in a program, a number of fine alternatives to AA are available—and none of them threaten "jails, institutions, or death" should you not thoroughly follow their path.

SMART Recovery

SMART Recovery (Self-Management And Recovery Training) Started in 1992, SMART is an abstinence-based, free, non-profit, self-help organization. Its methods are based on scientific knowledge, and evolve as scientific knowledge evolves. SMART stresses four key steps in recovery:

1. Building Motivation
2. Coping with Urges
3. Problem Solving
4. Lifestyle Balance

The SMART program centers on psychologist Albert Ellis's Rational Emotive Behavior Therapy (REBT). According to REBT, thinking creates your feelings and leads to your actions. This thinking/doing psychotherapy, REBT, helps members manage the beliefs and emotions that lead them to drink or use. By managing their beliefs and emotions, they empower themselves to quit.

Unlike AA, SMART meetings do not dwell on rehashing "war stories." Members are not much concerned with the past, except to learn from it. They focus on present-day events and the causes of self-destructive behaviors. The SMART groups provide a forum to discuss and find solutions for lifestyle changes and the problems members have with abstaining. Meetings are held once or twice weekly and members attend for as long as they feel the need. There are no dues or fees as each group is self-supporting through voluntary donations.

SMART views addiction as a bad habit and does not press its members to label themselves powerless or diseased. Participants are encouraged to take primary responsibility for their own recovery. There is no sponsorship or buddy system. Lay coordinators run SMART groups and each group has access to a professional advisor for added guidance. People concerned with other addictive behaviors, e.g., gambling, smoking, eating disorders, are welcome. On-Line meetings are conducted through the SMART web site. There are approximately 270 groups operating throughout the United States. To learn more about SMART:

SMART Recovery
7537 Mentor Avenue
Suite 306
Mentor, OH 44122
Tel: 440-951-5357
Fax: 440-951-5358
E-mail: srmail1@aol.com
Web site: www.smartrecovery.org

Secular Organizations for Sobriety (SOS)

Secular Organizations for Sobriety, also known as Save Our Selves, offers a self-empowerment recovery approach for those who are uncomfortable with the religious content of 12-Step programs. Founded in 1985 by James Christopher, non-profit SOS is an abstinence program, which centers on the "Sobriety Priority" statement: "I don't drink, no matter what." The organization encourages the scientific study of addiction in all its aspects and does not limit its outlook to one area of knowledge or theory of addiction. In November of 1987, the California courts recognized SOS as an alternative to AA when sentencing offenders to mandatory participation in a rehabilitation program.

SOS has a network of free, autonomous, non-professional local groups dedicated solely to helping individuals achieve and maintain sobriety. Each member is responsible for achieving and maintaining his or her own sobriety, without reliance on any "Higher Power." Members learn about the cycle of addiction and replace it with the cycle of sobriety. The organization also offers a variety of recovery "tools": printed materials, audio, and videotapes.

SOS deliberately offers no quality-of-life program and does not tell its members how to live. Consequently, SOS eschews "sponsorship"; instead, members approach each other as equals, respectful of diversity. There is no hidden agenda, as the organization is concerned with sobriety, not religiosity. SOS takes a reasonable, secular approach to recovery and encourages its members, through its freethought forum, to think for themselves and determine their own sets of values.

The organization has no opinion on outside matters and does not wish to become entangled in outside controversy. SOS seeks only to promote sobriety amongst those who suffer from alcoholism or other drug addictions. Each group is self-supporting through contributions from its members and refuses outside support. SOS guards the anonymity of its membership and the contents of its discussions from those not within the group.

SOS members keep their own personal journal of recovery, a specifically designed workbook covering 52 weeks of the year. Since drinking or using is never an option, members take whatever steps are necessary to continue their Sobriety Priority lifelong. Here are the SOS Guidelines for Sobriety:

To break the cycle of denial and achieve sobriety, we first acknowledge that we are alcoholics or addicts.

We re-affirm this truth daily and accept without reservation-one day at a time-the fact that as clean and sober individuals we cannot and do not drink or use, no matter what.

Since drinking or using is not an option for us, we take whatever steps are necessary to continue our Sobriety Priority lifelong.

A quality of life, "the good life," can be achieved. However, life is also filled with uncertainties. Therefore, we do not drink or use regardless of feelings, circumstances, or conflicts.

We share in confidence with each other our thoughts and feelings as sober, clean individuals.

Sobriety is our priority, and we are each responsible for our lives and our sobriety.

SOS stresses that its groups offer "support without dogma." Christopher's book, *How to Stay Sober* describes his own "recovery without religion" and includes strategies for the formation of secular support groups. For additional information, or to subscribe to the organization's quarterly newsletter contact:

SOS National Clearinghouse
The Center for Inquiry-West
4773 Hollywood Blvd.
Hollywood, CA 90027
Tel: 323-666-4295
Fax: 323-666-4271
E-mail: sos@cfiwest.org
Website: www.secularsobriety.org

Women for Sobriety (WFS)

Founded in 1976 by Jean Kirkpatrick, Ph.D., Women for Sobriety is both an organization and abstinence program dedicated to helping women overcome alcohol dependence and other addictions. WFS is non-profit and derives its operations money from group donations, sale of literature, speaking engagements, workshops and outside contributions.

The WFS "New Life" program centers on the "Thirteen Statements of Acceptance." Designed to empower women, the Statements are far removed from the ego-deflating 12-step teachings of AA. They are non-religious and stress members' strengths and building self-esteem. The New Life program is based on:

- Positive thinking
- Metaphysics
- Meditation
- Group Dynamics
- Pursuit of health through nutrition

Behavioral changes are encouraged through:

- Positive reinforcement (approval and encouragement).
- Cognitive strategies.
- Letting the body help (relaxation techniques, diet and physical exercise).

The WFS program concentrates on learning new self-enhancing behavior rather than using fear, reproach, and dependencies to control old destructive practices. Until the founding of WFS, it was assumed that any program for recovery from alcoholism would work equally well for women as for men. WFS came forth with the belief that women alcoholics required a different kind of program. While the physiological recovery from alcoholism is the same for both sexes, WFS focuses on the unique emotional needs of recovering women.

The ideal size of a group is from six to ten women, small enough so that every participant has a chance to be involved in discussions. Groups are run by a WFS-certified moderator who is well versed with the program and WFS philosophy. Moderators must have a minimum one year of recovery. Meetings are held at least once a week and do not exceed ninety minutes.

Jean Kirkpatrick also founded Men For Sobriety (back in the days when there were no programs such as SOS and SMART). There are very few, if any, active MFS meetings at present.

For additional information:

WFS (or MFS)
PO Box 618
Quakertown, PA 18951-0618
Tel/Fax: 215-536-8026
Tel: 800-333-1606
E-mail: NewLife@nni.com
Website: www.womenforsobriety.org

Rational Recovery (RR)

Founded in 1986 by Jack Trimpey, RR is a for-profit organization that features total abstinence recovery education. RR offers hospital services, seminars, counsel, literature, and a video and audiotape recovery series. "There is no disease of addiction," says Trimpey, and "complete recovery is nothing more or less than secure abstinence." There are no group meetings or reliance on Higher Powers.

Rational Recovery uses a Structural Model of Addiction. This Model divides the brain in two sections: the "beast" brain of addiction and the rational brain. By using Trimpey's process called Addictive Voice Recognition Technique, (AVRT™) the rational brain averts the "beast's" addictive urges. These urges are termed the Addictive Voice. Additional insights into the addictive voice concept can be found in Patrick Fanning and John T. O'Neill's recovery book, *The Addiction Workbook: A Step-By-Step Guide to Quitting Alcohol and Drugs*.

Trimpey explains AVRT™ in his book, *Rational Recovery: The New Cure for Substance Addiction*. He also travels the country teaching a course in AVRT™. RR's web site contains extensive information about the organization and its methods.

Rational Recovery Systems, Inc.
PO Box 800
Lotus, CA 95651
Tel: 530-621-2667
E-mail: rr@rational.org
Web site: www.rational.org/recovery

LifeRing

Officially organized in 1999, LifeRing Secular Recovery is chartered as a nonprofit corporation. It is dedicated to serving recovering alcoholics/addicts, and persons involved in relationships with them, and the general public, by holding meetings and public forums, and by publishing and disseminating educational materials related to alcoholism, addiction, and recovery therefrom. The core unit of LifeRing is the recovery meeting. Meetings (both on-line and in person) are autonomous except in matters affecting other meetings and the organization as a whole. LifeRing bases its program on the "Three S" philosophy: sobriety, secularism, and self-help:

1. Sobriety: Nothing is allowed to interfere with staying abstinent from alcohol and other drugs.
2. Secularism: LifeRing welcomes people of all faiths and none. Participants' spiritual or religious beliefs, or lack thereof, remain private. LifeRing supports recovery methods that rely on human efforts rather than on divine intervention or faith healing.
3. Self-help: In LifeRing, the key to recovery is the individual's own motivation and effort. The main purpose of the group process is to reinforce the individual's own inner striving to stay clean and sober.

LifeRing is a freestanding organization overseen by a seven-member board of directors composed of recovering alcoholics/addicts with a minimum of two years clean and sober. It is not affiliated with any other organization and is independent financially, legally, and organizationally. LifeRing is supported through the voluntary donations of its members and by literature sales. LifeRing directors and officers are not compensated for their services; all work is voluntary.

The only requirement for membership in LifeRing is a desire to abstain from the use of alcohol and illicit or non-medically indicated drugs. As in AA though, a break in abstinence means a loss of stature. A board member, for example, who knowingly breaks abstinence, must resign immediately. This errant director may stay on with LifeRing as a rank-and-file member, but he or she must resign the board at once and reset his or her sobriety time clock back to zero. By "sobriety," LifeRing means complete abstinence from alcohol and illicit or non-medically indicated drugs.

To learn more about LifeRing, its methods or to obtain a meeting schedule:

LifeRing Service Center
1440 Broadway Suite 1008
Oakland, Ca 94612-2029
Tel: 510-763-0779
Fax: 510-763-1513
E-mail: service@lifering.org
Web site: www.unhooked.com

Appendix C

What About Moderation?

Studies clearly show that certain individuals categorized as problem drinkers, heavy drinkers and, yes, "alcoholics" have successfully moderated their drinking. This unnerves disease theorists who insist that crossing the line into alcoholism leaves only one solution: abstinence. While *Overcoming Your Alcohol, Drug and Recovery Habits* is intended for those who want to quit for good, we must consider the option of moderation.

Generally, people who are able to eliminate the harmful effects of their drinking without quitting entirely are in somewhat good emotional and physical health. They won't concede to abstinence, but they will try moderation. Others, without programs, interventions, or treatment, simply cut back. Whether these people are "real alcoholics" is the sticking point with the disease theorists. "Real alcoholics" aren't supposed to be able to moderate. The fact is, some can.

In their groundbreaking book, *The Miracle Method: A Radically New Approach To Problem Drinking*, addiction researchers and authors, Scott D. Miller, Ph.D. and Insoo Kim Berg, MSSW, relate how their formal training in addiction treatment didn't mesh with their own life experiences and clinical observations. Flying in the face of their disease/treatment training, Miller and Berg's research chronicles many people who have independently quit severe addictions to booze, or have successfully learned to moderate. They witnessed this even in their own families. None of their loved ones resorted to formal treatment or AA meetings. There was no dramatic moment or life-changing revelation which led to their new attitude toward booze. They didn't need to "hit bottom" or turn their lives over to the "higher powers" of Bill Wilson's recovery religion. Please read this excerpt from Miller and Berg's book where they discuss their findings on moderation and quitting:

It had been drilled into our heads that no one who has the "disease of alcoholism" can stop drinking without treatment. Indeed, at one time or another in our careers both of us had read what Vernon Johnson, one of the leading authorities in the field, had written on this very topic: "Unless the chemically dependent person gets help, he or she will die prematurely. Chemical dependency is progressive [and] this means that it always gets worse if left untreated."

Perhaps, we both reasoned initially, our relatives were simply not real alcoholics or, in Johnson's words, "chemically dependent." However, we both had abandoned this thought long ago, given the chronic nature of our relatives' problems and the very real pain that alcohol had caused our families. If any persons fitted the picture of "alcoholic," they certainly were our relatives.

To complicate matters further, Insoo [Berg] related that her father had continued to drink socially throughout the remainder of his long life. This, we agreed, was supposed to be impossible since, as Johnson also pointed out, "once a person becomes chemically dependent, he or she remains so forever."

In short, we had to conclude that neither of us had any real idea about how our relatives had managed to stop [moderate] their drinking. They just simply seemed to go from having a serious drinking problem one day to not having that problem the next day. Both of them had somehow accomplished the theoretically impossible.

Could you accomplish the "theoretically impossible," too? Just as you'll never know if you have the talent for drawing if you don't pick up a pencil and try, you'll never know if you have the ability to drink sensibly if you don't pick up some moderation tools and try. Unfortunately, before most do try, they have been exposed to self-sabotaging recovery group movement propaganda: false notions of addictive disease, powerlessness, and the fantastic claims of addiction "experts" such as Vernon Johnson.

If you've already tried to moderate, but have failed, your failure means one of three things:

1. You are not following the correct methods.
2. You are using incorrect methods.
3. You are among those who, for whatever physical/psychological reasons, can't do it.

If sipping a drink or two over the course of an evening is your goal, moderation programs are good places to begin. But they can be harder than quitting: counting and measuring drinks, adjusting for body weight and food intake, tracking drinking days and non-drinking days, charting drinking patterns, attending meetings—all this and more, just so you can drink a beverage that your body does not need.

Even if you stick to these programs, don't think times like vacations or New Year's Eve mean that you can overdo it. Getting loaded isn't part of the package. Forget about experiencing the deep alcohol-induced pleasure of your former drinking days. Program guidelines are designed to keep blood alcohol levels extremely low. Remember, these are moderation programs.

Here's a tip: Develop a state of mind that abhors intoxication and strongly desires to be in control. This fundamental concept is essential to attaining and maintaining a temperate lifestyle. What's more, moderate drinkers are confident in their ability—they know they can moderate. Unless you come to know this at a gut level, don't expect success with moderation.

Indeed, failed attempts at moderation programs often lead problem drinkers to the conclusion that for them, quitting for good is the next step. But only you can decide when enough is enough.

How much time are you willing to devote to successfully integrating the moderate use of booze into your life. Six months? A year? Two years? Is moderation in your best interest and worth the time and effort? Are you reaping any benefits? Is the program essential to maintaining peace of mind? Is it contributing to your overall happiness? Are you consistently able to moderate? To help you make your decision, I've listed three nationally recognized moderation programs that could hold the key for you or for a loved one. You'll also find helpful books on this subject in the Suggested Reading section. Good luck.

Moderation Management (MM)

Founded in 1994, MM is now under the microscope. Founder Audrey Kishline was convicted in 2001 on vehicular manslaughter charges stemming from a drunk driving incident. "It's coming true," RGM members exclaim. "It's jails, institutions, or death for those who don't thoroughly follow our path." But Ms. Kishline *was* following their path. After several years of successful moderation, she began (during a particularly stressful period) experiencing persistent trouble moderating and had abandoned MM to rejoin AA two months prior to her drunken crash. (She had been a member of AA for years, and had been subjected to a 28-day rehab stint as well, prior to founding MM.)

Kishline always stressed that MM is not for everyone. It is geared for the problem drinker, not the "true alcoholic." Nor is it intended for former dependent drinkers who are now abstaining. As an organization, MM states that individuals who are not able to successfully reduce their drinking should find an abstinence-only program or remain in MM and choose abstinence as their goal. Additionally, MM is forthright in informing such people of their options. This includes SMART, RR, SOS, WFS, LifeRing and AA.

Based on sound principles, Moderation Management is a behavioral change program and national support group network. MM empowers individuals to accept personal responsibility for choosing and maintaining their own path, whether moderation or abstinence. MM promotes early self-recognition of risky drinking behavior, when moderation is an achievable goal.

MM is a viable alternative to abstinence only programs (there is an introductory 30-day no-booze policy). It makes sense to people who desire help in eliminating the harmful effects of their over indulging. Indeed, MM guidelines stress that moderate drinkers should not experience any health, personal, family, social, job-related, financial, or legal problems due to alcohol. And that a moderate drinker:

- Considers an occasional drink to be a small, though enjoyable, part of life.
- Has hobbies, interests, and other ways to relax and enjoy life that do not involve alcohol.
- Usually has friends who are moderate drinkers or nondrinkers.
- Generally has something to eat before, during, or soon after drinking.
- Usually does not drink for longer than an hour or two on any particular occasion.
- Usually does not drink faster than one drink per half-hour.
- Usually does not exceed the .055 percent blood alcohol concentration moderation drinking limit.
- Feels comfortable with his or her use of alcohol (never drinks secretly and does not spend a lot of time thinking about drinking or planning to drink).

202 • James DeSena

The nine steps of Moderation Management are:

1. Attend meetings (local groups or online) and learn about the program of Moderation Management.
2. Abstain from alcoholic beverages for thirty days and complete steps three through six during this time.
3. Examine how drinking has affected your life.
4. Write down your life priorities.
5. Take a look at how much, how often and under what circum stances you used to drink.
6. Learn the MM guidelines and limits for moderate drinking.
7. Set moderate drinking limits and start weekly "small steps" toward positive lifestyle changes.
8. Review your progress and update your goals.
9. Continue to make positive lifestyle changes, help newcomers to the group, and attend meetings as needed for ongoing support.

But ask yourself one question: Does the MM program, (or the idea of moderation in general) appeal to you, or to The Parasite? In other words, if you're thinking, "I can still get bombed now and then," translate that to "The Parasite wants me to get bombed now and then," and you'll know MM is appealing to The Parasite, not you. And if the introductory no-booze policy sounds unreasonable, then The Parasite is clouding your judgment for sure.

The Moderation Management program and Kishline's book, *Moderate Drinking: The Moderation Management Guide*, are valuable alternatives to the addiction treatment industry's "one size fits all" approach. To obtain a meeting schedule and learn more about MM:

HRC
22 W. 27th St.
New York, NY 10001
Tel: 888-561-9834
E-mail: mm@moderation.org
Website: www.moderation.org

Drink/Link

Founded in 1988 by Donna Cornett, Drink/Link Alcohol Moderation Programs are internationally recognized as the first clinically proven moderation programs in the United States. Designed for early-stage problem drinkers, for-profit Drink/Link offers an affordable seven-week home study program which guarantees reduced alcohol consumption.

The program includes a free 50-minute phone evaluation, Cornett's book, *7 Weeks to Safe Social Drinking: How To Effectively Moderate Your Alcohol Intake*, her booklet, *The Herbal & All-Natural Moderation Tips*, a motivational tape, nutritional supplements, the Drink/Link Drinking Diary and Drink Graph, Saliva Alcohol Tests and step-by-step instructions for the entire seven-week program. For an additional fee, a more intensive telephone counseling program is available. This provides seven hours of moderation counseling with a certified Drink/Link counselor. For more information:

Email: info@drinklinkmoderation.com
Website: drinklinkmoderation.com
Tel: 888-773-7465
Fax: 707-537-1010

DrinkWise

DrinkWise is a brief, confidential educational program based on over 20 years of successful clinical research conducted at the Addiction Research Foundation in Toronto, Ontario. This affordable program is for people with mild to moderate alcohol problems who want to eliminate the negative consequences of their drinking. A for-profit enterprise, DrinkWise helps clients eliminate drinking problems by reducing their drinking or stopping altogether. It is not for those who are severely dependent and/or experience withdrawal symptoms that require treatment approaches beyond the educational. The DrinkWise True/False Self-Evaluation Test helps clients decide which is better form them: moderation or abstinence.

The DrinkWise program is flexible. It includes a one-hour assessment, then four one-hour private sessions, or five two-hour group sessions, or four 40-50 minute telephone sessions or four one-hour telephone sessions. Each of the formats includes a three- and nine-month follow-up. Each DrinkWise counselor has a master's degree in social work, nursing, or health education and has extensive training and experience in alcohol education. The State of Michigan Office of Substance Abuse Services licenses the program.

The DrinkWise Program for Impaired Drivers provides assistance and education for individuals who have been arrested for driving under the influence of alcohol. An initial interview determines the type of counseling needed, after which the client may enroll in one of two brief DrinkWise formats with a specialized focus on drinking and driving. With the client's permission, written follow-up is sent to the court or attorney who made the referral to DrinkWise. The Impaired Driver Program is currently available in the in-person format only.

To learn more about the program and DrinkWise treatment locations:

M-Fit DrinkWise
University of Michigan Health System
2850 S. Industrial
Suite 600
Ann Arbor, Michigan 48104-6773
Website: www.med.umich.edu/drinkwise/
Tel: 800-222-5145
Fax: 734-975-1138

Recommended Reading

Charles Bufe. *Alcoholics Anonymous: Cult or Cure.* (See Sharp Press, 1998)

James Christopher, SOS Sobriety: The Proven Alternative To 12-Step Programs, (Prometheus Books, 1992)

James Christopher. *How to Stay Sober: Recovery Without Religion.* (Prometheus Books, 1988)

Jerry Dorsman. *How to Quit Drinking Without AA: A Complete Self-Help Guide.* (Prima Publishing, 1998)

Albert Ellis, Ph.D & Emmett Velten, Ph.D. *When AADoesn't Work for You: Rational Steps to Quitting Alcohol.* (Barricade Books, 1992) Recommended for its cognitive techniques.

Herbert Fingarette, Ph.D. *Heavy Drinking: The Myth of Alcoholism as a Disease.* (University of California Press, 1988)

Rebecca Fransway, AA Horror Stories: True Tales of Misery, Betrayal and Abuse, (See Sharp Press, 2000)

Marianne Gilliam. *How Alcoholics Anonymous Failed Me.* (Eagle Brook, 1998)

Robert Granfield & William Cloud. *Coming Clean: Overcoming Addiction Without Treatment.* (New York University Press, 1999)

A. Thomas Horvath, Ph.D. *Sex, Drugs, Gambling & Chocolate.* (Impact Publishers, Inc. 1999). Recommended for its cognitive techniques.

Audrey Kishline, *Moderate Drinking: The New Option for Problem Drinkers.* (See Sharp Press, 1994)

Michael Lemanski. *A History of Addiction & Recovery in the United States.* (See Sharp Press, 2001)

G. Alan Marlatt, Ph.D., JA Tucker, DM Donovan, Editors. *Changing Addictive Behaviors.* (Guilford Press, 1999)

G. Alan Marlatt, Ph.D., Judith R. Gordon, Ph.D., Editors. *Relapse Prevention.* (Guilford Press, 1985)

Scott D. Miller, Ph.D. & Insoo Kim Berg, MSSW. *The Miracle Method: A Radically New Approach to Problem Drinking.* (W.W. Norton & Co., 1995)

Scott D. Miller, Ph.D. & Insoo Kim Berg, MSSW. *Working With the Problem Drinker: A Solution-Focused Approach.* (W.W. Norton & Co., 1992)

Heather Ogilvie. *Alternatives To Abstinence: A New Look at Alcoholism and the Choices In Treatment.* (Hatherleigh Press, 2001)

Stanton Peele, Ph.D., Archie Brodsky, Mary Arnold. *The Truth About Addiction and Recovery.* (Fireside, 1991)

Stanton Peele, Ph.D., Charles Bufe, Archie Brodsky. *Resisting 12-Step Coercion: How to Fight Forced Participation in AA, NA, or 12-Step Treatment.* (See Sharp Press, 2000)

Ken Ragge. *The Real AA: Behind the Myth of 12-Step Recovery.* (See Sharp Press, 1998)

Jeffrey A. Shaler, Ph.D. *Addiction is a Choice.* (Open Court Publishers, 2000)

Philip Tate, Ph.D. *Alcohol: How to Give It up and be Glad You Did.* (See Sharp Press, 1997). Recommended for its cognitive techniques.

Jack Trimpey. *Rational Recovery: The New Cure for Substance Addiction.* (Pocket Books, 1996)

Jack Trimpey. *The Small Book: A Revolutionary Alternative for Overcoming Alcohol and Drug Dependence.* (Delacorte, 1992) Recommended for its cognitive techniques.

Joseph Volpicelli and Maia Szalavitz. *Recovery Options: The Complete Guide.* John Wiley & Sons, 2000)

Bruce W. Wilshire. *Wild Hunger: The Primal Roots of Modern Addiction.*(Rowman & Littlefield, 1999)

Index

188 • James DeSena